Puppy Mill Dogs SPEAK!

Happy Stories and Helpful Advice

By Christine Palm Shaughness
with Chris M. Slawecki

Dedication

This book is dedicated to the dogs who still suffer in puppy mills so that the American public can have furry friends.

I pray for the day when the dichotomous nature of our relationship with dogs becomes more balanced instead of the huge gap we have today between revered family member and cash crop.

—*Chris Shaughness*

Contents

Introduction	i
Chapter One: What's That Around My Neck?	
Leash Walking	1
Chapter Two: This Grass Feels Funny	
Grass & Other Surfaces, and Housetraining	15
Chapter Three: Don't Watch Me While I Eat	
Eating Habits	27
Chapter Four: How Do You Walk Up and Down These?	
Steps	39
Chapter Five: Take Cover!	
Noises	51
Chapter Six: Who Are You?	
Greeting People	63
Chapter Seven: Hands Are Good Things	
Being Touched	95
Chapter Eight: I'm Never Going Back in a Cage Again	
Crate Training—Yes or No?	109
Chapter Nine: Hold It!	
Walking Through Doorways	119
Chapter Ten: Don't Make Any Changes	
Consistency and Routine	123
Chapter Eleven: Get Me Outta Here!	
Flight Risk	129
Chapter Twelve: It's Time for Progress	
Leadership and Training Principles for All Dogs	137

Chapter Thirteen: Health Issues of Puppy Mill
 Breeder Dogs.. 157

Chapter Fourteen: Health and Behavior Issues of Puppies
 from Puppy Mills.. 165

Afterword 173

Resources.. 177

Acknowledgements... 179

Beginnings

On Buddy's initial visit to the university, he stepped gingerly onto the campus lawn and rolled around on his back. The look of complete bliss on Buddy's usually stoic face moved Ron to tears. For the first time in Buddy's four-year life, this sweet dog enjoyed a frolic in fresh cut grass...

Buster did not have much opportunity—or spirit—to run in his former life. His first few attempts, tentative but hopeful if clumsy gallops, led Chris to tell me that Buster runs like he "just discovered that he has legs." These moments of joy and others like them have made their journey over the past year worthwhile...

Ann could hardly contain her happiness when Penny stood patiently while Ann put the harness on her. Knowing this was a tremendous accomplishment for Penny, Ann still could not resist giving Penny a little pat. Penny was more receptive to being touched from that day on...

Introduction

Welcome to the world of rescued puppy mill dogs! Puppy mills are places where dogs are bred for profit, with little regard for the health of the puppies and no regard for the dogs who breed to produce them. These dogs, often called "line workers" or "breeding stock," spend their entire lives in cages. They never know a life beyond waking and sleeping in wire cages, lying in their own wastes, deprived of loving human touch.

Because of legislative and social pressures, some puppy mills are surrendering their breeder dogs to rescue organizations and shelters, who try to rehabilitate and prepare them for adoption.

Once in a home, these dogs need to learn how to be human companions. They must be housetrained and learn how to accept human touch and affection, negotiate stairs, walk on a leash, even how to play.

Puppy Mill Dogs SPEAK! is a book about dogs who were used as breeders in puppy mills and the incredible adopters who give these unique creatures a second chance. The book is a collection of their stories as well as tips for helping these—and all—dogs to adjust to living with people in their homes.

Decades ago, pet dogs in this country were mostly bred in American homes, surrounded by children and other pets. Maybe your family mutt jumped the fence, sauntered around the neighborhood, and delivered a surprise back home eight weeks later. Your family would place a "Puppies for sale" ad in your local newspaper or put a sign in your yard, and sell your puppies from your home.

Today, we see an increased demand for purebred, novelty breeds, or "designer dogs." Some people will see a celebrity or someone in their neighborhood with a certain breed and become fixated that they simply must have that kind of dog, too. They don't care where their dog comes from, just so long as they get the dog they want. Other people just don't understand, or don't care, where many of these dogs come from.

Each year, millions of dogs are euthanized in shelters, yet people still buy pet store puppies. If people truly love dogs as much as we say, why aren't we doing something to stop this? Why insist on getting a puppy instead of rescuing a dog from euthanasia? Why does it seem like so many people who claim to so deeply love dogs, really don't?

Certainly, some breeders are reputable and invest time and money into producing quality puppies. But others are not so upstanding. Many commercial breeders see breeding as a way they can make a profit from this demand for dogs. So do many farmers who consider a dog to be just

Introduction

another crop, just another animal in the barnyard. Such breeders have no idea of what these dogs are capable of, what jobs they can be trained to do or how much love they have to share. Or if they know, they don't care. Dogs are just the assembly line that produces the next crop of profit.

These places that crank out puppies like an assembly line, regardless of the health or behavior problems of the puppies or their parents, are known as puppy mills.

In many puppy mills, certain dogs are selected to be "breeder dogs"—the males and females used to produce the puppies. Breeder dogs are generally kept in cages and are brought out for only one purpose: Breeding. They live confined, often trapped among their own wastes. For many, their only human contact comes when they're brought out to breed or if they are lucky enough to have someone toss some cheap food into their cage.

The first time that I saw breeder dogs, I didn't know they were breeder dogs. The whole puppy mill issue had not yet come to the public forefront, and animal shelters and rescues were referring to them as "farm dogs." They were "shy."

My first client who turned out to be a breeder dog was adopted from Delaware Valley Golden Retriever Rescue (DVGRR) in Lancaster County, Pennsylvania—the "Puppy Mill Capital of the East." DVGRR is a volunteer non-profit group that rescues at-risk or otherwise displaced

Golden Retrievers and places them for adoption. (You can learn more about DVGRR in the "Resources" section at the back of this book.) The dog was named Stella, was later renamed Penny, and you'll read her story in this book. Her adopter was told that she was "very, very shy." She was having extraordinary problems with Stella and I was stumped trying to help her. All I could do was pull from my knowledge about dog behavior as a dog behavior counselor, and I was at a loss.

But the first dog that I knew was a rescued breeder dog was a young Golden Retriever who DVGRR had just brought in from the puppy mill farm. They put a leash on her and she dropped straight to the ground. It was like she had no legs. She was frozen in terror, pancaked on the ground. You could tell that she was in such a tremendously panicked state. She went between pancaked and crawling on the ground, then whirling around on the leash, trying to escape it. I had worked with submissive dogs before. Many crouched down and rolled onto their backs in the classic posture of submission. But I had never seen a sight like that.

I approached her in my usual confident way. On purpose, I did not look directly at her and I did not advance head-on, which dogs can consider aimed threats. When I got close enough, my outstretched hand offered her a treat. You would think that a dog would happily gobble the treat then stick around to be petted, but not this one. She did not care about the food. She knew she could go nowhere while she was on

Introduction

that leash, so she dropped to the ground and froze. She was practically paralyzed with fear. Unlike most other fearful dogs who may try to bite you if you attempt to touch them, she simply shut down.

This was just the most heartbreaking thing I had ever seen. It was so far away from what a dog should be, that happy, waggy-tailed Golden Retriever that you'd picture in your family home. She instinctively knew what a kennel was and bolted toward the kennel door. She was so obviously terrified that we just allowed her to run in. She found the safest spot in a corner that she possibly could, and sat there trembling. It was horrible.

Most breeder dogs have no names. Some may have numbers tattooed on them; others wear chains that embed painfully into their neck as the dog grows. When brought out to breed, they're grabbed roughly by the scruff of their neck, yanked painfully by their legs, or lassoed around their neck by a rope or cord then dragged out. Females are frequently strapped down into a device called a "bitch hitch" that holds her still so she can be impregnated.

Many puppy mills house hundreds of dogs. In order to remain inconspicuous, their owners "de-bark" the dogs so that the noise of their barking does not give away their puppy mill. How are most breeder dogs "de-barked"? The owner holds the dog's head back and thrusts a metal pipe or sharp stick down the dog's throat to crush their vocal chords. No anesthesia.

Many puppy mill owners consider breeder dogs to be useless when they can no longer reproduce their next for-profit crop. These "useless dogs" are bludgeoned, drowned (often called "going to the bucket"), shot to death, or simply abandoned and left to starve and die alone. The more fortunate breeder dogs are surrendered to dog rescue organizations. Others are confiscated when the puppy mill is raided by the local humane society, and delivered to these rescues. More and more dogs are being rescued as public awareness about puppy mills grows. Every so often a breeder might even place a small "free to a good home" ad in the same local newspaper you'd use to sell your own puppies.

But how can breeder dogs learn to trust a human after what they've gone through? Certainly, there are degrees of agonizing treatment that these dogs have endured—from least to most cruel, if nothing else—which is evident from their behavior. Some dogs recover and learn to trust relatively quickly. Others never fully recover.

Most "normal dogs" you meet with and through your friends and family have the benefit of being introduced to positive human contact at a very young age (known as "socialization"). We often assume that dogs just naturally bond with and trust humans, but this is not true. A puppy needs a certain amount of positive human handling, of socialization, early in their development to create that bond. Without it, pups can grow up to fear humans.

Introduction

The behavior of a poorly socialized dog is essentially that of a wild animal. They cannot comprehend the possibility of a human touch being pleasant or that it might be nice to live in a comfortable home. Poorly socialized dogs become flight animals who desperately dash away at the first unfamiliar noise like a frightened deer running away from its predator.

As a behavior counselor, I encounter quite a few scared breeder dogs who have trouble dealing with living in the world outside of their cage. When I began to volunteer as the behavior counselor at DVGRR, where I served for several years, I did extensive research through stacks of books and journals and the internet, and even contacted other animal behavior specialists. But I could find no information about living with rescued breeder dogs or how to help them live like "normal dogs." Other animal behavior specialists and dog trainers rarely work with dogs that have such issues, and when they do see these kinds of dogs, they have no idea what to do for them. They call them "shy dogs" and often recommend euthanasia.

Since then, DVGRR staff and I have had the distinct pleasure to work with these rescued breeder dogs. We have learned so much from these special dogs. When these rescued dogs are subsequently adopted, I have had the even greater privilege following their progress as they adapt to life in a home. As you will read later, most have never negotiated stairs, or heard a vacuum cleaner or hair dryer, or walked on a leash before coming to the rescue. Some are afraid to walk on smooth surfaces like hardwood or linoleum floors.

Watching these dogs learn and overcome their handicaps with the aid of their new "parents" is a gift for me. I have learned so much from these dogs and their people. The stories of these dogs are not complete without the stories of the people and families who adopt them.

Living with an adopted breeder dog certainly has its ups and downs. I don't know why anyone would want to go through some of the struggles other than our basic human need to be compassionate. It's possible that these breeder dogs evoke such strong sympathetic feelings in many of us—the abuse is written all over their sad, scared faces—that we can't resist wanting to help such a pathetic looking animal. I guess it's just the compassionate nature and need to help in our human DNA. I know people who have adopted three and four rescued breeder dogs at a time. I don't know how they do it. I'm not even sure that I could do it, so tremendous is the patience required to heal some of these dogs.

But the rewards of seeing these rescued dogs blossom into happy pets are forever gratifying. Rescued puppy mill breeder dog adopters are a special group of people, as you will read in the following stories. Of course, not everyone can deal with the unique issues that these dogs can bring into their lives. Some people try but just can't do it and sur-

Introduction

render their adopted dog back to the rescue. I have met more than a few people who came to the very sad conclusion that they could not properly care for a dog who demands so much of their time, effort and emotion. That's okay—because as word spreads of the travesty and horror of puppy mills, more and more people are opening their homes and hearts to these rescued survivors.

Typical and Not So Typical Behaviors

Most breeder dogs share common characteristics that you typically do not find in dogs who have been raised by caring humans. These behaviors often result from their living trapped in a cage with no exposure to loving treatment from humans in the atmosphere of a home. Everyday things that we all take for granted can be new experiences for breeder dogs.

Constant if not obsessive fear of sudden movement, of strangers, and fear of going through doorways, are consistent characteristics of breeder dogs. Like all dogs, they also have their own personalities, so they will be able to cope with things better or worse, depending upon that personality. Some rescued puppy mill dogs have such high anxiety that they cannot deal with the change from the puppy mill. Like the first time I met that female Golden, for example: I tried to get her to walk on a leash but no amount of coaxing could get her to her feet. Even luring her with food was out of the question. I could tell rather quickly that she needed to be left alone and given time to recover from her stress, so I ran back in the direction of her kennel. She darted past me and ran inside, back into the only security she had ever known. It's really sad to say, but being in a puppy mill may even be better than being out for dogs like this, because the world outside is such a scary place for them.

The following chapters detail these unique behaviors through the stories of rescued puppy mill breeder dogs. You will also find tips for working with their typical and not-so-typical behaviors, plus a discussion of the health issues of the dogs and puppies who come from puppy mills.

Introduction

Tips for Teaching Your Dog to Walk on a Leash

♥ Breeder dogs kept in cages were usually dragged around by the scruff of their necks or lassoed with a rope when it was time to be handled, such as for breeding. They can be very fearful of having anything around their necks as a result.

♥ It takes time and patience to get such dogs accustomed to walking on a leash. At first, most of them will freeze in place and refuse to move. A body harness generally works best. Take it slow: Place the harness on your dog and allow him or her to walk around the house wearing it for short periods of time. After your dog is comfortable wearing the harness, attach the leash and allow the dog to drag it around the house. After your dog is comfortable wearing the harness and leash, pick up the leash and begin to lead your dog around the house.

♥ Use a body harness or a head halter instead of a collar. If your dog cannot use a body harness, the Gentle Leader® head harness offers another good option.

♥ Introduce the harness slowly by allowing the dog to sniff it.

♥ Give yummy treats to your dog as you introduce the harness.

♥ Allow your dog to wear the harness for very short periods of time around the house.

♥ Gradually increase the wearing time until your dog is not afraid of the harness.

♥ Introduce a leash using the same method as the harness, slowly.

♥ Allow your dog to drag the leash around the house to become accustomed to it.

♥ Do not use a retractable leash until your dog is comfortable with a regular, flat leash.

Chapter One

As I drive up the long gravel driveway, I see an old wooden sign bearing names of dog breeds scrawled by hand: "Boxers, Yorkies, Jack Russells, Golden Retrievers, Poodles"...

WHAT'S THAT AROUND MY NECK?

Leash Walking

You can frequently distinguish breeder dogs by their fear of walking on a leash. With rare exceptions, breeder dogs are never let out of their cages during their time in puppy mills. The dogs' breeders may have used a cord to capture the dogs when it was time to breed them, leading them to fear anything resembling a leash. Some breeders may have selected one or two dogs to parade out in public, to give potential puppy purchasers the notion that they are reputable breeders, all the while hiding most of the other dogs behind closed doors. They pick a few dogs to show as "the mother and father dogs" when people arrive to look at their puppies. But even with this exposure to having something tied around their necks, the dogs' leash walking experiences are minimal.

Breeder dogs might react like a wild horse who has just been lassoed. They may become severely frightened and try to run away. Others simply lie down and refuse to move. No amount of pulling or coaxing will help when they shut down out of fear like this. Adopters of rescued breeder dogs find that this issue is one of the most challenging, and requires a great deal of creativity and patience to overcome. Some dogs refuse to walk. Others may begin to walk, but then they stop and won't get back up. Buddy was one of these dogs.

Buddy, the English Gentleman

I first met Buddy at DVGRR, about two weeks after his arrival. I brought him from his kennel into the room where I evaluated dogs who had recently arrived at the facility. This day was a milestone for Buddy, the first time he had been inside anything that resembled a home.

Buddy would not come over to me. He nervously scanned the expansive room and then began to occasionally spin in circles, a sign of high anxiety. I sat on the floor near him. He did not run from me; he froze in place. I slowly inched my way to him and was finally able to touch him, although his discomfort was clearly visible. I lightly stroked him for only a minute or two, not wanting to place too much stress on him. Buddy accepted my touch but was relieved when I moved away—then the spinning resumed. He was even more thankful when I led him back to his kennel and the only safety he knew. When I opened the kennel door, Buddy scooted in and lay as far back in the corner as possible.

Buddy arrived at DVGRR after four years of captivity in a puppy mill. The breeder surrendered Buddy because he was no longer interested in breeding Golden Retrievers. Public demand was increasing for Golden Doodles—the cross-breeding of a Golden Retriever and a Poodle—and the breeder thought he could make more money with this type of dog. Buddy was now free from his role of stud.

What a beautiful, wonderful stud he must have been. Buddy is the color of rich mahogany with the personality of a perfect English gentleman. Settled into his new home eight months later, he has impeccable manners as he greets you with his lifted paw and solemn expression. Never pushy, he waits patiently for recognition and lays his head in your lap in anticipation of your well-deserved affection.

The month that Buddy stayed at DVGRR was a period of stressful transition. After having lived only in a crate for all his life, Buddy's new home in a larger, clean kennel at DVGRR was strange to him. Four times a day, he was coaxed to grassy and mulched areas that felt unfamiliar to his paws. He had never been out of his crate, after all, to learn what grass feels like. He was brought to a large fenced in area but was unaware of how to enjoy this freedom. When one of the staff members threw a tennis ball to him, Buddy just looked at the ball, innocent of what a ball was or what to do with it.

Donna and Ron adopted Buddy from DVGRR on July 4, 2006—Buddy's Independence Day. Finally, he could know what it was like to live in a home with people who love him. But the first several months were not without problems. Sadly, Buddy couldn't initially realize how lucky he was. After he hesitantly walked through the front door of his new home, Buddy continuously paced in the kitchen area for almost three hours. Exhausted, he sat but refused to lie down. He finally closed his eyes and began to list to one side but was still afraid to lie down and sleep because of the newness of his environment and unfamiliarity with the two strangers in his presence.

What was he supposed to do in this new place? He had never seen anything like it, with wood floors that felt strange to him, unfamiliar rugs and furniture, and unusual noises. Surprisingly, Buddy willingly ate his dinner without reservation then settled nervously onto a soft mat to spend his first night in his new home. Eventually, Buddy would feel safest in the kitchen, where Ron and Donna also spent much of their time.

Buddy's first days in his new home were scary for him. Every noise startled him. He often bolted from an unfamiliar sound; sometimes he froze in place. A little coaxing with some cheese or chicken jerky usually overcame his fears, yet Buddy still would not venture far out of the kitchen area.

Neighborhood walks were the biggest problem for Buddy, Ron and Donna. Buddy walked nicely on the leash right from the start, but often stopped and froze at every mailbox. One time when Ron and Donna were walking with Buddy and he refused to move, Donna had to walk back home—nearly a mile—get their car, drive back to pick up Ron and Buddy, and drive them home. Several times, Ron had to pick up Buddy and carry him over the threshold into the house because Buddy was afraid of walking through doorways—no small feat because Buddy weighed over sixty pounds! During this time, Ron seriously considered returning Buddy to DVGRR. Ron is a professor and department chair at a university and simply had to be at work on time. If Buddy refused to budge during their morning walk, it made Ron late and created a great deal of stress for all.

What's That Around My Neck?

That's when Ron called me for advice. I recommended using cheese or another type of treat to lure Buddy into walking again. Most importantly, I recommended replacing Buddy's collar with a body harness, so that the leash was not pulling on his neck. Originally, Buddy was walked wearing his regular flat collar. When he stopped during his walk, Ron and Donna found it very difficult to get him moving again by pulling on his leash and collar. This made him even more distressed: Many breeder dogs had either been pulled by their collars or grabbed by the back of their necks, making them very sensitive to anything around their necks. Luckily, the harness and some cheese did the trick!

If Ron and Donna already had another dog in their home, Buddy could have benefitted from having a "guide" to show him around. Often, breeder dogs feel more comfortable and can relax when they are with other dogs. Ron and Donna were allowed to adopt Buddy because he had progressed nicely and was considered to be more social than most breeder dogs by the time he was ready for adoption. In retrospect, Ron, Donna, and Buddy may have had an easier time if they had another dog for Buddy to learn from.

On their usual daily walking route, a small white dog who lives at a house down the street barked aggressively at Buddy. Although this dog was contained in a yard with an invisible fence, Buddy was very frightened and froze in his tracks whenever he encountered this dog. On one occasion, instead of turning around and going back home, Ron and Donna picked him up, Ron on one end and Donna on the other, and carried Buddy past this house with the barking dog. Imagine how silly they must have looked and felt! But this was the only way to get Buddy past this property.

Buddy froze every time he approached this house during their walk, even if that small dog was not outside. Ron and Donna cleverly thought of a way to get Buddy moving: They brought along handfuls of cubed cheese and threw them in front of Buddy, several feet down the sidewalk, to entice him to keep moving. Fortunately, Buddy is very food motivated: He scrambled to get the cheese as Ron and Donna continued to toss more ahead of him, until they eventually passed by the house of the barking dog. In time, Ron and Donna did not need to throw cheese to get Buddy to move along; instead of hesitating or freezing in place, Buddy quickly runs past this house now!

After just four days of living with Ron and Donna, Buddy began accompanying Ron to work at the university. Without hesitation, Buddy entered the building and seemed to know exactly where to go. Although passing through a doorway was usually a scary thing for Buddy, he confidently walked through the doors to get to Ron's office, then made himself at home by lying in the middle of the room. This certainly was inconsistent behavior for a dog who was fearful of being in a home! Ron and Donna could only surmise that Buddy knew the scent of the office because he smelled it every day when Ron came home from work. It was familiar to Buddy and he had quickly learned to associate this scent with Ron's happy arrival home. Buddy swiftly established his position in Ron's office and now greets visitors with a polite "handshake." Students and faculty love to visit Buddy and are immediately taken with how sweet he is.

After a couple of weeks, Ron and Donna noticed that Buddy wanted to crawl into the dishwasher. You don't see many dogs do that! Buddy was persistent but Ron and Donna discouraged him. It didn't take long for Ron and Donna to figure out that Buddy thought the dishwasher was like the cage he used to live in and made him feel more secure.

Eight months after being adopted, Buddy still shows signs of his abhorrent past. He does not like to venture far from his safe zone in the kitchen and frightens easily when he hears an unusual noise. When startled in the house, Buddy may try to flee outside. Ron and Donna must be very careful to keep Buddy gated or harnessed and leashed when the doors may be opened to the outside.

One day, as they were bringing Buddy into the house after a walk, Ron accidently bumped a small gate in the foyer after Buddy was inside and his leash had been removed. The falling gate frightened Buddy who then turned and bolted back through the open doorway. Donna, who was still on the front porch, was forced to lunge and grab Buddy to stop him from fleeing. She fell in the process, but neither was hurt and Buddy was safely returned inside. Now Ron and Donna are very cautious about noises and open doors, and realize that Buddy may always have this issue.

The challenges certainly were many for Buddy, Ron and Donna. But the triumphs and moments of joy made it all worthwhile. On Buddy's initial visits to the university, he stepped gingerly onto the campus lawn and rolled around on his back. The look of complete bliss on Buddy's usually stoic face moved Ron to tears. For the first time in Buddy's four-year life, this sweet dog enjoyed a frolic in fresh cut grass. He had gone from being tentative about the feel of grass during his stay at DVGRR to blissfully rolling around in it.

Another joyful moment of triumph came when Buddy jumped into the car without coercion. For many months, Ron usually had to coax Buddy into the SUV using a ramp into the back of the car, or he had to pick Buddy up and place him in the car. But one December day, as they were preparing to get on their way to the university, Buddy just hopped into the car! He now effortlessly jumps in and out and loves his car rides. After all, Buddy has a job as "ambassadog" at the university and needs to be there to receive all of the loving attention from his many admirers! He has brought many smiles to students, staff and faculty as he walks through the halls or on the campus.

Because breeder dogs have rarely or never walked on a leash, it is vitally important that you make their initial leash-walking experiences positive and happy. Using the proper equipment and methods for teaching your dog to walk nicely on a leash can make a huge difference.

First, the wrong collar may increase the dog's anxiety and fear of walking. Any metal choke chain or prong collar is inappropriate for a breeder dog (and any dog, for that matter). These collars constrict around the neck and cause discomfort. Any physical discomfort increases the dog's feeling of anxiety. The more anxiety the dog feels, the more fear the dog associates with walking.

Instead, I recommend a harness that goes around your dog's chest. The best types are the harnesses where the leash attaches to the front of the harness across the chest. If your dog pulls, the harness gently holds the dog back without causing any tightness around the neck. Your next best option is a head halter, which has a loop that goes over your dog's nose. If your dog pulls, the halter gently pulls the dog's head around to the side. Some dogs may be afraid of these types of collars, and they must be introduced slowly and carefully to your dog.

Because so many breeder dogs are spooked by a leash, please ensure that whatever collar or harness you use is securely in place so that your dog cannot slip out. Breeder dogs will run away as far as they can go in order to escape any unpleasant situation. As you will read later, it can be very difficult to catch them.

You may need to take a very slow approach when placing the harness or head halter on your dog. Some dogs may be fearful of this equipment and it may take days or weeks before your dog will allow you to place the equipment on him or her. Begin by showing your dog the equipment while offering a very high quality treat like canned chicken or cheese. Watch your dog's reaction when you show your dog the equipment. If your dog appears fearful, give more treats but discontinue the exercise after a few minutes. Try again later, and do this several times a day. Continue showing your dog the equipment while offering treats until your dog appears more relaxed. Gradually begin placing the equipment over your dog's head as you are still feeding treats.

When you do get your dog to walk, a short leash is better than a long or retractable leash. A shorter leash allows you to have more control over your dog—the longer the leash, the further away from you your dog will be, and the less likely to respond to your instructions. A four or six foot leash is preferable. Your dog may not want to walk when you put the leash on. Your dog may either sit still with feet planted firmly, or may lie down fearfully and refuse to get up, or may desperately try to get away from the leash. If your dog reacts in any of these ways, you will need to introduce the leash in the same way as with the harness and head halter above.

A very slow desensitization to the leash may be necessary before you attempt to walk with your dog. Let your dog smell the leash as you offer treats. Drape the leash over your dog's back and offer treats. Lay the leash over your dog's paws so he or she gets accustomed to the feel of the leash on his or her fur. All these actions will help show your dog that the leash is nothing to fear.

Once your dog is walking without fear, keep your dog by your side and constantly praise your dog while he or she is walking nicely. Should your dog stop walking or begin to falter, simply call out a happy "Let's go!" and keep walking. If you stop, your dog will learn that it's okay to stop. Guess what? Your dog has trained you! Train your dog to watch you for cues instead.

On the other hand, if your dog pulls you on the leash, you need to be the one to stop! Do not proceed until your dog lets up on the pulling. Allowing your dog to pull just teaches him or her that they are leading the walk. If your dog pulls, simply reverse directions. Keep doing this until your dog understands that he or she must watch you to determine where you are going. You lead the walk.

Now, some very important words about things you must not do. Some dog trainers still teach a dog how to walk nicely on a leash by doing "leash pops." The trainer uses a metal choke collar and when the dog pulls, the trainer gives a quick jerk on the leash so that the collar tightens around the dog's neck. This method is supposed to show your dog that if they pull, they will be threatened with punishment; just like it sounds, this method will evoke fear in your dog. If you use this method on a breeder dog, your dog may shut down and not walk at all. Leash pops not only sound terrible—they really are terrible to a fearful dog.

Finally, there is a horrible tactic that some dog trainers and even breeders still advocate called "hanging" or "helicoptering." In this tactic, you are instructed to pull up on the leash and lift your dog's front feet up off the ground when your dog pulls on the leash. This is intended to demonstrate that you are the leader, and that your dog is helpless to go any further without you. Helicoptering takes this tactic to a greater extreme by lifting all four feet off the ground, and holding your dog there until he or she stops squirming. Both tactics are horribly detrimental to a fearful dog's psyche. This will only teach your dog to fear leashes even more.

Sadly, many people who really should know better still believe that these methods are valid and should be used to train all dogs. Experienced dog trainers and other people who think that they know how to train dogs may recommend that you work with your dog this way. Remember that knowing how to train a dog and understanding dog behavior are distinctly different skills.

These tactics are no ways to form a trusting relationship with your dog, adopted or otherwise. If anyone, professional or not, suggests using these methods, please refuse.

What's That Around My Neck?

Housetraining Tips

Housetraining certain puppy mill breeder dogs can be challenging. But use these six principles, and often a little creativity, and you can overcome this challenge together. The end of this chapter gives greater details on each of these steps.

♥ Use a consistent door/location.

♥ Create a consistent schedule.

♥ Never let your dog out of your sight.

♥ Reward, never punish!

♥ Be patient!

♥ Thoroughly clean up all accidents.

Chapter Two

The farmhouse is old yet well cared for, and laundry hangs on a clothesline to dry in the country breeze. It is a bucolic scene where one envisions life is simple, happy, and ideal...

THIS GRASS FEELS FUNNY

Grass & Other Surfaces, and Housetraining

What would it feel like to always be in a cage? Early in their development, puppies get accustomed to feeling certain sensations under their paws. Anything else feels strange and uncomfortable. This is called their "substrate preference."

Most puppy mill dogs never feel anything other than wire crate or maybe straw under their paws. Their first venture onto a strange surface can be very distressing to these dogs. Grass, wood flooring, tile, linoleum, or concrete can feel different or unusual; because the surface is unusual, the dogs are unsure of themselves while walking on it. It may even feel like we feel when we're walking on ice—unsteady, off-balance, and very afraid. Some dogs might refuse to walk at all. Others may step gingerly and slowly.

Of course, some dogs are more sensitive than others in their paw area, as you know if you've ever owned a dog who disliked walking in the rain or snow!

Maggie, Who Runs Like the Wind

Sally and Dan Capozzelli already had two Goldens, Penny and Rubin. But they knew that they had room in their hearts and home to rescue another one. In April 2007, they attended DVGRR's monthly Adopt-a-Golden Day.

Sally and Dan both spotted a beautiful yet withdrawn female named Fluff among the sea of sad homeless Golden faces. She was a reddish-blonde color with very thick, somewhat curly hair, and a light face. The hair on her tail was so profuse and wavy that it braided into a thick, dense weave, and obviously had been very neglected prior to her coming to rescue. When Sally and Dan approached Fluff, she buried herself behind her handler's white lawn chair and dropped to the grass in a panic attack. She was the terrified antithesis of the friendly, outgoing Golden Retriever, yet she touched Sally's and Dan's hearts.

Sally and Dan knew they needed to help this sad little girl. They inquired about Fluff's background, knowing nothing about puppy mill survivors. DVGRR staff did not sugar coat their replies. They gave Sally and Dan the honest facts on the challenges of bringing home a dog who had never lived in a house or had positive association with people prior to coming to DVGRR. When Sally and Dan asked my opinion, all I could do was pass along the words spoken by other adopters of rescued breeder dogs: "It's one of the most challenging things I've ever done but certainly one of the most rewarding." The Capozzelli family would definitely agree.

This Grass Feels Funny

Sally and Dan have since changed Fluff's name to "Maggie" and during one of our follow-up visits, little more than one year later, they were all eager to show me how Maggie had progressed. I watched Sally give each dog their dinner, then ask them to sit and stay—first Rubin, then Penny, and finally Maggie. All waited patiently. Sally gave the "okay" signal and in unison all three chowed down! Sally's face glowed with unmistakable pride, especially for her Maggie, who once upon a time would not eat when anyone (especially Dan) was in the room.

Maggie remained terrified of Dan for a long time after adoption. She would flee from him when he entered the room and never approached him. This made caring for Maggie very difficult, especially getting her to go outside to go to the bathroom and then getting her to come back inside. Consequently, Sally had to be Maggie's caretaker. But every day, Dan sat on the floor or in the grass, his hands outstretched and armed with slices of sharp cheddar cheese and deli ham, in hopes of gaining Maggie's trust.

Even the day that they brought her home gave Sally and Dan a small glimpse into Maggie's issues: They watched a DVGRR staff member lift Maggie into their car. She had shut down in fear. Cars were unfamiliar to her, as were these two new people, and she had no idea how to jump into the car. Arriving home posed the same problem in reverse: How to get Maggie out of the car? Penny and Rubin to the rescue! They excitedly jumped into the car to greet their new sister. Maggie forgot her fears as she joined in the fun and leaped out of the car to follow her new friends.

But not so quick. To get into the house, Maggie needed to walk up a few steps then through a doorway, all things she feared. Instead of forcing her, Sally and Dan led her to the large, fenced-in back yard with Penny and Rubin. For the large part of the afternoon, Maggie paced the yard, unable to relax and enjoy herself.

Grass was still new to her, because during her years at the puppy mill, Maggie may have never been let out of her cage. The soft green blades that seemed so inviting felt uncomfortable and unsure beneath her paws instead. She could find no comfort moving, or standing still, on the grass. A dog enjoying a leisurely snooze in the soft cool grass paints a great picture, but grass made Maggie nervous because it was still new to her.

This house, these people, and those dogs, were all new to her too. Again, without Penny and Rubin, Maggie would not have come inside. Finally, she followed them in, and found the place that was to be her "safe spot." The Capozzelli's family room is just inside the French doors off of their second story deck, and is decorated with lots of dog pictures and memorabilia, a testimony to their love of dogs.

Maggie went directly to a corner next to the sofa where she could hide unnoticed. This would be the site of many frustrating family moments, when she would not come out, but also of many triumphs, such as the day we taught Maggie to "sit" by having her back up against the corner. This corner is also where Maggie began to learn to love and trust Dan. With his deli cheese and ham, Dan sat with Maggie in this corner, patiently hoping she would overcome her fear of him.

Three short months after they had adopted Maggie, Sally needed to stay in the hospital for a few days. How could Dan care for Maggie, visit with Sally, and get to work on time? As the saying goes, necessity is the mother of invention. Dan called on one of their other dogs, Penny, to help him. Dan was able to leash Maggie and Penny together on a double leash, and the three of them took collective walks, instead of allowing Maggie to run loose in the fenced backyard where Dan would have trouble catching her. It worked, thanks to Penny for making Maggie feel more secure, and thanks to a little ingenuity on Dan's part.

Finally, after six months, Maggie learned to trust Dan (and, of course, to think of him as a walking deli!). Dan was quick to show me how Maggie is comfortable around him. Every night, while Sally and Dan relax on the family room sofa, Maggie sits right next to them with her head on Dan's knee. This is one of the rewards of adopting a rescued puppy mill dog.

It is such a difficult thing to understand—and to not take personally—when a dog like Maggie shows fear of a kind and loving man such as Dan. He so obviously adored her and eventually won her heart with his unending streams of love, time and patience—and sharp cheddar cheese. All Dan needs to do now is open the refrigerator door and Maggie comes running! With time, a little training, and lots of companionship from Rubin and Penny, Maggie is confident and happy.

Housetraining

One of the most challenging behaviors of breeder dogs, or dogs who have lived all their lives in cages, is that they are not housetrained and are often very difficult to housetrain.

Dogs have an innate instinct to eliminate in a spot away from where they sleep and eat. They are naturally clean animals.

Breeder dogs have had to squelch this instinct because they have had no choice. They were never let out of their cages, and their cages were not big enough for them to eliminate at one end and to sleep and eat at the other end. They were never shown a routine of going out to a grassy area to eliminate. The only way of life they've known was to constantly lie in their own wastes. So when these dogs find loving homes, it can be a challenge to re-instill their instinct for cleanliness. Crate training is the best way to housetrain a dog—but if the dog is deathly afraid of a crate, the process will be very difficult and challenging.

While Dan worked on winning Maggie's trust, their biggest challenge was ongoing: Housetraining. Sally and Dan were gone all day at work and they knew that Maggie was not housetrained. DVGRR recommended crate training her. Maggie was not thrilled with going in a crate but she went along with it. She seemed to settle down when Sally and Dan left for the day. But what a mess they discovered when they arrived home: Maggie had eliminated in the crate, ground the feces into the crate liner, and flung the rest out of the crate in all directions. She needed to be bathed, the walls needed to be scrubbed, and the crate liner needed to be washed—every single day.

After two weeks of this torture, Sally and Dan wondered if Maggie would be better off living with people who could be home most of the day. Thankfully, they called me for advice. We talked through some options and Sally and Dan came up with the idea of putting Penny and Maggie together in their very large master bathroom while Sally and Dan were gone. I suggested that they do a trial run for an hour or two. That did the trick! Everyone was happy. Sally and Dan no longer needed to spend an hour cleaning every night; best of all, Maggie felt more secure.

To see Sally and Dan now, it's difficult to imagine the challenges they faced when Maggie first came home. Today, Maggie looks like a happy "normal dog" with a few quirky exceptions. For one, she hesitates to come in from outside, possibly from the fear of doorways that so many rescued puppy mill dogs exhibit. This issue can be very frustrating for Sally and Dan; sometimes it can take an hour for Maggie to decide to come inside. Also, she shuts down in public places like the vet's office and on trips to the pet supplies store. Sally and Dan took Maggie for a trip to a local pet store to buy her a birthday present, thinking it was going to be fun for her. Instead of having a fun afternoon, Maggie wished to be back home in her safe place. She is still not comfortable in strange situations.

Walking on a leash is another issue that can be problematic for Maggie. Maggie pulls to come home, showing the same discomfort as she does in public places. Lastly, she has coprophagia—stool eating—

another common problem with puppy mill dogs. Sally and Dan must be vigilant in cleaning up their yard. But nothing overshadows the joy that Sally and Dan feel when they see Maggie acting out the puppyhood she was denied, as she sprints across their yard and rolls in their grass.

"Maggie," they shout together, "you run like the wind!"

Housetraining Tips

Housetraining certain puppy mill breeder dogs can be challenging. But use these six principles, and often a little creativity, and you can overcome this challenge together.

- ♥ Use a consistent door/location: Always take your dog out the same door and to the same place in your yard. Dogs are scent animals and recognize their own odors. Establish an area in your yard or wherever you regularly walk your dog and wait for him or her to eliminate there.

- ♥ Create a consistent schedule: Establish a routine, daily feeding and walking schedule. Do not deviate from this schedule, even on weekends. Take your dog outside to his or her designated spot immediately after each meal, immediately after awaking, and right before bedtime. Some dogs may need to go out every few hours.

- ♥ Never let your dog out of your sight: Until your dog is housetrained, do not leave your dog unsupervised in your house. Either use a crate to confine your dog when you cannot be there to supervise, or block him or her in a small area. This way, you will be able to catch your dog in the act of eliminating in the house and can immediately take him or her outside to their designated spot.

- ♥ Reward, never punish!: Should you see your dog beginning to eliminate in the house, interrupt the behavior with, "Ah, ah, ah—outside!" and take your dog outside. Never, ever scold your dog for eliminating in the house. Dogs do not understand when you stick their noses in their housetraining mistakes, or if you hit them when they have an accident. These reactions only teach your dog to fear you, and to eliminate in the house when you are not looking. Instead, use praise and treats when your dog eliminates when and where you want. The very instant that your dog begins to eliminate in this place, say, "Good dog!!!" with lots of enthusiasm, then reward with a treat when he or she is finished.

Housetraining Tips
(Continued)

♥ Be patient!: You now know that most puppy mill breeder dogs were never given the opportunity to eliminate away from their cages. So teaching them to go somewhere else may be a lengthy process. Some dogs will learn quicker than others; some may always have housetraining issues. Please be patient and continue to follow these six principles.

♥ Thoroughly clean up all accidents: Carpet cleaner alone is not effective to remove pet odors in the house. Use a pet deodorizer such as Nature's Miracle®.

This Grass Feels Funny

Tips for Getting Your Dog to Feel Comfortable When Eating in Your Presence

♥ If your dog accepts food from your hands, hand-feed your dog's meals.

♥ Sit on the floor with your dog's bowl in your lap and feed your dog one or two nuggets at a time. Yes, it's time consuming!

♥ When your dog is eating, ensure that noise is kept to a minimum. The environment should be quiet and calm.

♥ If your dog feels threatened by other dogs in the room while eating, ensure that all dogs are out of the room.

♥ Never scold your dog if he or she growls at you or other pets while eating.

♥ Consult a qualified pet behavior specialist if your dog shows aggression when eating.

Chapter Three

I see no one outside to help me, so I walk around the back of the house to the barn. It looks just as old and well cared for, with large heavy whitewashed doors and no windows. I call out, "Hello," but get no answer...

DON'T WATCH ME WHILE I EAT
Eating Habits

For most "normal dogs," the sight of food is a gloriously happy event that calls for joyous dancing and acting like goofballs. But breeder dogs may associate food bowls with unpleasantness: Metal food bowls may have been thrown into their cages, creating loud banging noises, or their breeders may have used food to lure the dogs in order to grab them. Feeding time may have been the only time that they saw humans, and under these conditions they formed a negative association between food and humans. Many breeder dogs are reluctant to eat when humans are nearby. They typically are not aggressive around their food bowl, but they freeze at the sight of people and won't eat.

However, some rescued puppy mill dogs can be highly food aggressive. The conditions at their mill may have forced them to compete with other dogs that may approach them while they are eating. This was their natural survival behavior if the dog was starving.

Ginger, the Sly Fox

Arriving at DVGRR's kennel facility was the beginning of Ginger's great new life. Ginger and her nine puppies were transported from a Missouri puppy mill by DVGRR staff along with another breeder dog and her brood of eight. For at least a month, Ginger, the other dog, and their 17 combined puppies, occupied the DVGRR education room. Thin and weak, Ginger was a good mom but was obviously weary of her role as a breeder. She tried to hide in a corner if anyone entered the room. She spent the next month weaning her pups while recovering from her ordeal of the past four years, and awaiting adoption.

Dawn Trautwein heard about Ginger and her puppies and volunteered to foster Ginger (a foster home provides a temporary place for a dog to live and learn while the rescue organization looks for the dog's permanent home). In April 2006, after Ginger's puppies found homes, Dawn brought Ginger in to live with her. Because she had many years of dog experience, Dawn believed that she was prepared to deal with the challenges of living with a dog who had not been socialized with humans or had never been exposed to life in a home environment. She was told that Ginger was a "shy dog," so Dawn read a book about "shy dogs" to learn more.

When Ginger entered Dawn's house that first day, she behaved more like a wild animal than a domesticated dog. Dawn had never seen a dog who had no dog-like qualities of affection and playfulness, but Ginger had neither. Everything terrified Ginger. She was extremely vigilant about her environment and watched Dawn's movements very carefully. Dawn felt like she was living with a fox, not with a shy dog.

Ginger stayed in her crate in the living room for those first few days. When Ginger began to venture out, Dawn sat in a chair and made great efforts to not look at Ginger, for any eye contact was enough to make Ginger flee back into her crate in fear. Dawn tried tossing food in Ginger's direction to lure Ginger closer, but this only frightened her more and made her slink back to her crate.

Patient waiting was the only tactic that worked for Dawn and Ginger. Dawn's patience paid off—within a week or two, Ginger managed to venture over to where Dawn was sitting and nosed her hand for a pet. Maybe Ginger wasn't quite a wild animal. Maybe there was hope.

Your Attitude

Dogs come with an inborn ability to read human facial expressions, vocalizations and even our emotions. When we're happy, they just seem to pick up on it and feel better themselves. Show your dog anger, impatience or frustration and they will know it, and recoil from you. So it is very important to convey an upbeat attitude when working with your breeder dog. Talk happily yet softly to your dog, and ensure that you do not raise your voice.

Like with any other dog, you will be tempted to lose your patience with your breeder dog from time to time. When you feel this way, it is very important, like with any other frustrating situation, that you make sure your dog is safe and comfortable, then take a break and walk away to settle yourself. You will make no progress together if your dog senses your frustration.

Find a friend or a support network of people who understand what you are going through, and talk it out.

Patience is supremely important. You will need to be able to spend time just sitting and waiting for your dog to come over to you. Some dogs will approach you in hours. Some may take months.

Even though Ginger had approached her, Dawn realized that she still needed to take it slow. From that day forward, Dawn established certain goals and expectations for Ginger while fostering her. First, Dawn required Ginger to be out of her crate for just an hour each day. This does not sound like much time, but for a seemingly wild animal now exposed to civilization, an hour must have felt like an eternity for Ginger. This short time out of her crate helped Ginger to face her fears instead of hiding from them.

Once Ginger began to venture out of her crate, she started to explore the house and found several hiding places. Ginger was never afraid of going up and down steps, so she would sneak upstairs to Dawn's bedroom and crawl under her bed. Then Dawn could not get her out! Dawn very cleverly placed paper grocery bags on the steps, which deterred Ginger from going upstairs. Not many dog owners must devise such strange and creative arrangements.

Dawn's second goal was for Ginger to walk nicely on her leash. This may sound easy, but not for a dog whose only leash experience was when the breeder lassoed her to breed her for more puppies. Ginger was terrified of collars and leashes as a result. This goal, walking on a leash, brought Dawn a great deal of frustration. Each and every noise scared poor little Ginger to death. Even the croaks of the spring peeper frogs in Dawn's woodsy neighborhood alarmed Ginger. Her reaction was to flail and whirl on her leash in a desperate attempt to retreat from the forbidding, wide open new surroundings. But Dawn would not tolerate

Ginger's nuclear reactions. When Ginger wanted to flee home in fear, Dawn simply remained calm and in control. With time, Ginger regarded Dawn's leadership as a sign that everything was fine. The use of a harness or head halter to walk Ginger also helped enormously, because it removed that restricted feeling from around Ginger's neck.

Throughout their summer together, Dawn tried several methods to help Ginger overcome her fears. It occurred to Dawn that she had been accommodating Ginger way too much, so Dawn decided to challenge Ginger more. Dawn had read a book that suggested leashing your dog and attaching the leash to your belt, so that everywhere you go in the house, your dog must follow. Dawn tried this technique for about a week but it was too much for Ginger to handle.

Mealtime presented another challenge: When her bowl was placed on the floor, Ginger would run from the room and not eat. Dawn had to feed Ginger by hand. Dawn realized that Ginger needed to push through this fear just as she pushed through her fears of getting out of her crate and walking on a leash. She decided to place Ginger's food bowl on the floor instead of feeding her by hand, thinking that Ginger would eat when she grew hungry enough. But Ginger's fear proved much greater than her hunger, and she would not eat for several days. Dawn resumed feeding by holding Ginger's food bowl. Ginger stiffened and remained very alert, and craned her neck into the bowl to eat. Sometimes she even stopped eating in mid-meal and ran from the room.

Through all of this, Dawn never considered returning Ginger to DVGRR. All these trials were difficult, but they seemed easier to bear because Dawn knew that she was only fostering Ginger. Dawn always assumed that Ginger would eventually go to someone else's home, so she was able to somewhat detach from Ginger because she was simply doing her job—preparing Ginger for that eventuality.

Dawn never realized just how attached she really was becoming to Ginger. At a subsequent DVGRR Adopt-a-Golden Day, Dawn sat on the lawn with Ginger as people greeted the dogs available for adoption. One lady showed interest in Ginger but then decided that she didn't like the way Ginger looked. Dawn was surprised at how hurt she was by this woman's rejection of Ginger. Her protective reactions made her exclaim to herself, "That's MY dog!" Dawn decided that very day to adopt Ginger as her own.

The same day that Dawn made Ginger's adoption official, she adopted another Golden Retriever from DVGRR and named him Jubil. Jubil's arrival helped Ginger tremendously. She had a pal to play with and learn from.

If anything frightens Ginger these days, she runs to Dawn's house. Dawn's entire house is now Ginger's safe place, although she has found several special, favorite spots. Ginger rarely goes into her crate anymore, unless Dawn asks her to. She prefers the bathroom floor or her big soft dog bed in the living room, and she sleeps beside Dawn's bed at night.

Gathering Stuffed Toys or Other Objects

Ginger loves to play with her friend Jubil but has still not quite caught on how to play with toys. She loves stuffed toys although she does not play with them. When Dawn throws her one, she runs after it, picks it up and places it in a special spot with all of her other stuffed toys, lining them all up very orderly. To Ginger, these toys are her puppies. She picks them up carefully and makes certain that they are all together in one safe place.

Mother breeder dogs do not leave their instincts behind when they are rescued from puppy mills. Most if not all of these rescued females recently had puppies; many may have been taken from their puppies, or had their puppies taken from them, before her pups were properly weaned. Some females are still lactating. These mother dogs feel the need to be a mother due to the hormones still lingering in their bodies, if not their many years of constant nurturing.

In the absence of puppies, some females like to gather objects—stuffed toys, towels, socks, and other articles of clothing—and bring them into their crate or safe spot when they come to live in their forever homes. Many will take stuffed toys that belong to their owners, or toys that belong to their new canine siblings. Some of their new canine siblings may not care for this behavior.

There is nothing harmful or "wrong" when a dog gathers toys and you should not discourage this behavior. However, while this act may appear to be very cute and endearing, it can also create stress between the newly adopted dog and the resident dog whose toys are being purloined. In several cases I worked with, the resident dog attacked the breeder dog for stealing their toys. Unfortunately, the best solution to stop such fighting was to remove everyone's toys. To avoid this type of conflict, take away all toys, or give your dogs toys only when they're separated, or supervised.

Some rescued breeder dogs eventually outgrow this practice. Others do not. You will have to assess your household, your dogs, and the severity of this situation, and decide if you should manage your dogs' toys.

The day I visited Dawn to interview her for this book, Ginger had accomplished another milestone. For the first time, she picked up a tennis ball, pawed at it, then pounced on it like it was a mouse. This is breakthrough behavior for a breeder dog—at last, Ginger was showing the puppy playfulness of which she was deprived when she was really a pup.

Ginger has attended several classes at a local dog training facility and has proudly received her certificate in beginning obedience. She still can have "puppy mill moments" of panic, especially around men and in situations where there are many people and a lot of activity. But Ginger never completely shuts down any longer, and she snaps out of it when Dawn tells her, "Let's go!" Dawn can even instruct Ginger to "go say 'hi'" to greet visitors to her home, and Ginger will come over for petting. She stands motionless and an experienced dog handler will recognize that Ginger remains a little uneasy, yet she has come such a long way from where she and Dawn began.

Ask Dawn if she would ever adopt another rescued breeder dog again, and she'll respond with an enthusiastic, "Absolutely!" However, this experience helped Dawn to realize that Ginger's recovery was all at Ginger's pace and that Dawn had very little control over the timeline. "It was a very humbling experience," Dawn agrees.

Walks

For a normal dog, a walk outside can be like a hunting trip or a scavenger hunt. Dogs love to explore sights and sounds, smell where other animals have left their marks, chase after small prey, and greet other dogs and people. But for a breeder dog, the outside world can be a very scary place. Fear of the unknown plus fear of leashes present an extremely frightening combination for these dogs.

Ultimately, a walk can be a great tool for helping your breeder dog to become more socialized and less fearful. The trick is getting your dog to overcome his or her initial fear of being leashed and taken outside.

Make sure you have the proper gear before you go out. Using a harness gives your dog a better feeling of security, ensures your dog does not escape, and minimizes the discomfort around your dog's neck. A short leash is vital because it will keep your dog from venturing too far from you; the closer your dog is to you, the more you will be able to guide your dog.

Always remember that your breeder dog has no idea what a walk is. If your dog is very afraid to walk outside, do not take the dog for walks too far from your home at the beginning. Your dog may decide to shut down and not move, and you don't want to have to carry your dog too far back home! Start with very short walks around your own yard. Observe how your dog seems to be handling these short walks: Is your dog's tail tucked under, or is it out in more normal position? Is your dog curious about its environment? Does it sniff the ground, the grass, the trees? Does your dog stop and refuse to keep walking? How often? All of these observations provide clues about how your breeder dog is adjusting to his or her new environment.

Don't Watch Me While I Eat

Tips for Teaching a Dog to Negotiate Steps

- ♥ Motivate your dog to walk up or down the steps by placing something or someone highly desirable at the top/bottom of the steps. Often, the presence of another dog incites the dog to run after it.

- ♥ If you have a staircase with only a couple of steps such as stairs off of a deck or porch, begin there instead of a large staircase.

- ♥ Take it one step at a time. Sitting at the bottom of the staircase, place some high value pieces of treats (cheese, bacon, liver bits, etc.) on the bottom step to get your dog to reach to get it.

- ♥ Gradually coax your dog one step at a time to reach for the special treats.

- ♥ Don't rush the process—just one step is a major accomplishment!

- ♥ To go down steps, if your dog is not too large, place the dog on your lap as you scoot down the steps slowly. Make sure you laugh while you do this so that your dog associates fun with going down the steps!

Chapter Four

The latch on the barn door is not bolted so I slowly pull the big door open, still looking for the owners. When it opens, a smell hits my nostrils so overpoweringly that I gag and want to run away...

HOW DO YOU WALK UP AND DOWN THESE?

Steps

How many of us take walking up and down stairs for granted? To a four-legged creature who has never been exposed to steps, it's an intimidating prospect. Try this experiment for yourself: Get down on your hands and knees at the top of a staircase, and look down. Place one hand on the next step, as if to come down the stairs. It doesn't feel very natural, does it?

This is what a dog feels the first time that he or she encounters steps as an adult. A staircase can be very scary to a dog who has lived his or her entire life in a cage; there are no steps in the natural world and they simply do not understand the concept. Most of our homes have steps somewhere, and teaching your dog how to navigate them is one of the main challenges of adopting a rescued breeder dog.

Lily, Queen of Agility

You don't hear very many dog owners admit, "It was pure hell for the first couple of months." But these were the very words spoken by Adele Hood when asked if she would ever adopt another rescued breeder dog. You must also know that Adele quickly concluded her statement with an upbeat, "But worth it!"

Lily lived her first four years in a Missouri puppy mill, producing litter after litter of puppies. Her body permanently bears witness to her past. Lily's apprehensive face reveals the scars of the abuse she endured, with spots of fur missing from her reddish-brown muzzle.

Lily arrived at DVGRR's kennel facility with her eight puppies in the early spring of 2006. She lived in the education room with Ginger, who we met in chapter three, and Ginger's nine puppies. When a person entered the room, Lily wearily leaned against the nearest wall for safety while her liberated little pups happily greeted each visitor. Lily seemed grateful for any break from the constant strain of motherhood that she had endured since she was less than one year old. If cornered, Lily stood perfectly still and allowed you to pet her, but she was obviously uncomfortable. Lily did not flee, but remained fearfully frozen in place in a trance-like state until left alone. Her head bowed down slightly and her eyes darted nervously from side-to-side to avoid eye contact.

Adele originally agreed to be Lily's temporary foster mom, to help Lily adjust to life in a loving home, in May 2006. Lily's first few weeks at Adele's home certainly were "pure hell," not just for Adele but for Lily, too. Lily ran away from everything. When she wasn't fleeing, she frequently froze in terror. Although very scared of her new environment, Lily followed Adele everywhere in the house with one exception—upstairs, because Lily was afraid to go up steps. Adele began sleeping in the living room to provide Lily with the comfort of knowing that Adele was nearby. Lily needed to be near Adele, but she would not let Adele get close enough to pet her.

How Do You Walk Up and Down These?

Lily eventually found her safe place on Adele's living room and family room sofas. Lily would follow Adele from room to room, then quickly perch herself on one of these sofas to gain the best vantage point to watch Adele. Lily observed Adele's movements very carefully, always cautious and ready to flee. She ran off if Adele tried to approach her. Adele noticed another peculiar issue with Lily: She automatically sat down, with that constantly worried look on her face, whenever someone approached her. Clearly, after years of forced breeding, Lily was protecting her rear area from invasion. Feeding time was disturbing, too. Lily would not eat if Adele was anywhere near her food. So Adele left Lily's food bowl on the floor then disappeared to another room to give Lily the privacy she needed to eat.

Throughout their first few months together, Adele gradually lured Lily closer with treats and praise. Adele recognized that they were making progress and was pleased. However, she also recognized that Lily was nowhere close to being what people would consider a "normal dog." Yet Adele grew to love Lily unconditionally. As Adele later phrased it, because, "No one in their right mind would adopt a dog like this," Adele adopted Lily as her own.

Once Lily started accepting Adele's touch, their relationship grew much smoother. Adele was able to start working on taking Lily for a walk. The sight of a leash can make most dogs dance with delight: "It's time for a walk!" But not Lily—whenever she spotted the leash, she ran and hid. With lots of time, patience, love, praise, and treats, Adele gradually taught Lily to not fear, and then to walk nicely on, her leash. There were many days that Lily refused to continue walking, but now she loves her daily walks and even heels perfectly by Adele's side. In fact, Lily now seems happier when she is outside and more nervous in the house.

After Lily overcame her fear of leashes, Adele decided that Lily was ready to attend school. Adele picked a class for shy and untrusting dogs at a nearby dog training facility. She enrolled in Confidence Class, where dogs and their people learned different exercises designed to help the dogs overcome their fears. One session simply showed the attendees how to touch and massage their dogs in order to relax them, while another taught the dogs basic obedience skills such as "sit" and "come."

The most momentous class was the session when the instructor took everyone outside into the field used for agility. Agility is a sport for dogs that involves running the dogs through obstacle courses of jumps, tunnels, and ramps, at their handlers' direction. That day, the instructor led the class to the A-frame, a wooden structure composed of a narrow ramp up and another narrow ramp down to the ground, in the shape of an "A." For an agility competition, the A-frame is set up high off the ground. But for this class, the instructor kept the ramps low to the ground so as to not further intimidate these already fearful dogs. The idea was to lead the dogs onto the A-frame slowly, so that they could gradually conquer their fear.

The instructor asked Adele to walk up the A-frame with Lily trailing behind on her leash. Adele slowly inched up the ramp, with Lily loyally following. Much to Adele's surprise, Lily continued to follow her until they walked to the top and down the other side. But the next step was even more challenging: Lily was to walk up and down the A-frame by herself.

Lily took her first step up to the ramp with Adele still walking alongside her. Lily watched with her characteristically worried look while Adele encouraged her to continue. After only a minute, Lily climbed up to the top and then in a flash ran down the other side. Lily had done it! Lily dashed to Adele for a big hug. With tears of pride in her eyes, Adele praised her beautiful Lily while the whole class clapped in amazement. That night, Adele sent a proud eMail to all of her friends and to DVGRR about Lily's wonderful accomplishment.

Each and every class presented Lily with a new challenge. The scariest class came when the instructor had everyone exchange dogs. This meant that Lily and Adele had to be apart! When an unfamiliar man took Lily's leash, Lily regressed. She pulled on the leash to go back to her safe spot on her dog bed, and then went into a trance. She sat frozen on her bed no matter how much the man coaxed Lily to come to him. She allowed him to stroke her, but kept her eyes diverted from his and her brow remained furrowed with anxiety. Lily breathed a sigh of relief when Adele returned to her.

One of the best things that Adele learned in Confidence Class was a technique called TTouch,[1] short for Tellington Touch, to help Lily grow more comfortable with being petted. With TTouch, you use your thumbs to rub in small, light stroking circles upon your dog's body to

---

[1] Tellington-Jones, L. (1993). The Tellington TTouch: A Revolutionary Method to Train and Care for Your Favorite Animal. New York, New York: The Penguin Group.

relax your dog. Adele used TTouch to get Lily accustomed to being touched, and Lily loved it. Adele and Lily now have a TTouch bonding session every day, and have added brushing to their daily repertoire. Lily drinks in this loving attention.

Adele also adopted a friend for Lily a few months after adopting her—Brina, another female Golden Retriever with a happier disposition. She was not a breeder dog. Brina's confident personality helped Lily venture to places that she otherwise would not have gone. Before Brina, Lily did not like to go outside into Adele's fenced-in yard by herself. But Brina's exuberance coaxed Lily out to play with her new friend. Lily also never barked before Brina arrived, but quickly began to chime in whenever Brina barked.

The addition of her playmate brought out Lily's true personality, which is playful and silly, at least with other dogs. The normally stoic dog with the constant cautious look on her face turns into a mischievous pup when she plays with Brina, so much that Brina often gives Lily a warning growl to calm things down a little!

The girls share their treats and peanut butter every day. Adele laughs as she watches Lily bounce up and down in anticipation of her epicurean luxuries. You would never know that Adele could not even get near Lily for those many long months before. Lily bounces around when she knows it's time to go for a ride in the car, too.

Once a week, Adele drives with Lily to a local skilled nursing and physical therapy center to visit with the patients. Lily is surprisingly un-

How Do You Walk Up and Down These?

afraid of elevators, wheelchairs, walkers, or crutches, but is extremely frightened of canes. Lily stands very quietly while the patients pet her, and Adele keeps the petting time to a minimum. The exposure and socialization that Lily receives in this new environment and to different people are invaluable. Adele is also working on Lily's fear of canes: Adele keeps a cane hanging on the wall so that Lily can see it and occasionally takes it down from the wall to lay it on the floor and even gently touches Lily with the cane sometimes.

Adele learned another fun confidence-building activity at Confidence Class. Adele set up an obstacle course in her home, using furniture and that cane of which Lily is so fearful. Adele tells Lily and Brina to stay in the family room and then clusters chairs close together between the family room and living room, laying the cane in the middle. Then Adele calls for her girls to come find her in the living room. Brina bounds confidently through the course, while Lily, not wanting to be left alone, haltingly follows Brina in between the various objects. When Lily reaches the cane, she gingerly steps around it. Awaiting Adele happily cheers as Brina and Lily accomplish their feat. This exercise is important for Lily because it helps her to become less fearful of new situations and changes in her environment.

Lily has made tremendous strides, but Adele still has concerns about her emotional state. Lily is very, very attached to Adele, and even after two eight-week sessions of Confidence Class remains fearful of other people. Adele cannot hand Lily's leash to anyone else without Lily going into her trance and freezing. Lily never tries to flee; she always looks to find Adele. This, of course, concerns Adele, who hopes that her sweet little dog will eventually learn to trust other people. There may come a time when Adele will need to be away from home and someone else must care for Lily.

Lily now sleeps in Adele's bed with her at night, and even sneaks upstairs occasionally to swipe a stuffed animal off the bed. Adele believes that patience, not allowing yourself the luxury of getting upset, love and praise, lots of understanding, and realizing that your dog is watching you more carefully than you can imagine, have all brought her and Lily together to where they are today. Who knows what will happen next? Maybe one day Lily and Brina will have another friend to help nurture into a happy dog.

Steps

Teaching your dog to walk up and down steps may be a slow process. Some dogs will be more fearful and resistant, while others need only to be shown a couple of times. Motivation is the secret: Your dog needs to really want to get to the other end of the stairs! So, when you decide to teach your dog how to walk on steps, find something that is very motivating for your dog: A high value food such as canned chicken, steak, or something else that your dog loves but rarely receives; your dog's breakfast or dinner; a toy or a bone (if your dog plays with toys or bones); or even another dog that your dog enjoys being with.

How Do You Walk Up and Down These?

Begin, literally, with one step at a time. It is best to practice on a small set of stairs with only a couple of steps, or very wide steps. Closed-in staircases are less threatening than steps which are open (especially steps that are open at the back). Teaching a dog to go up the steps is generally easier than going down, so start your dog at the bottom of the stairs with the intention of climbing up. Place the food (or whatever motivator you decide to use) on the first or second step and lead your dog to take it. Give soft and happy praise when your dog does. Most puppy mill breeder dogs will stretch out their front ends to get to the food but leave their rear legs planted in place. You may need to hold the food in your hand and lure your dog closer to the steps, to coax him or her to move their entire body closer.

Keep your training sessions short and happy. Remember that just getting your dog to take the food from the bottom step may be a great accomplishment! End each training session on a happy note. You may want to consider several short sessions every day, instead of pushing your dog too quickly. The goal is to get your dog to associate good things with overcoming the challenge of steps.

Once your dog begins to show a comfort level with taking the motivator from the bottom step, gradually move it to the next step, or lure your dog with it as you slowly walk up the steps. Your presence on the upper steps may be enough to motivate your dog to walk to you. Each dog is different and may require an individualized approach.

If luring is not working and your dog still resists, you may need to physically move your dog up and down the steps to get the process started. Wrap a large bath towel under your dog's belly like a sling. Hold the ends of the towel and lift, to elevate your dog one step at a time; guide your dog's paws to "walk on" the steps while you lift. (Depending on the size of your dog, you may need more than one person to help with this exercise!)

One adopter of a breeder dog thought of this creative solution to teach her dog to go down steps: She sat at the top of the steps with her dog on her lap, and held onto her dog as she slowly scooted down the steps, one step at a time. Talk happy and laugh as you scoot down (thinking of how you look will make you laugh anyway!) so your dog associates happiness with this activity.

If none of these techniques work, consider hiring a dog trainer or behavior specialist who is knowledgeable about puppy mill breeder dogs to help you.

How Do You Walk Up and Down These?

Tips for Helping Your Dog to Tolerate Noises

♥ The least little unexpected noise will scare most breeder dogs. Select a noise, such as a door bell, which your dog will frequently hear and cannot avoid. A technique called counter-conditioning will gradually acclimate your dog to scary sounds.

♥ Counter-conditioning involves getting your dog to think that "good things happen" when it hears the sound. Start by taking your dog somewhere in the house where the door bell can be heard very slightly.

♥ Have someone outside ring the bell, and at the same time, give your dog a jackpot of high value treats! Repeat this process for a very short period of time and, by all means, discontinue if your dog appears too stressed or refuses to eat the treats.

♥ If your dog tolerates the sound from a distance, gradually move closer and repeat the process. Very gradually!

♥ This method can be used for any sound that frightens your dog.

♥ Never, ever force your dog to repeated exposure to scary sounds by trapping him or her.

Chapter Five

But the sounds of dogs whining and barking inside encourage me to press on. Holding one sleeve over my nose to protect it from this odor, I enter the barn and stare in utter disbelief...

TAKE COVER!

Noises

Life in a barn was probably pretty noisy for puppy mill dogs, but it was mostly the sounds of barking and crying dogs, snorts and brays of the other animals, and the occasional shout from the breeder. Sounds of machinery may have been a part of their lives, too. But you won't find a hair dryer, washing machine, garbage disposal, or vacuum cleaner, in a barn. You won't hear the din of a blender, food processor, or coffee grinder, either.

These are all new and often frightening sounds to a dog who lived a very sheltered life in a puppy mill cage. These dogs may run fearfully from each noise in search of their safe place to hide. They might also associate the loud clatter with whomever or whatever was close by when they heard the noise, which can develop brand new fears. Of course, some dogs may not be bothered by such noises because of the sounds that he or she may have been exposed to. A loud lawn mower or tractor might have been part of their previous way of life, and one to which they became easily accustomed in their new one. Every dog's experiences with noise will be unique.

Take, for example, one breeder dog who came to her new home after living in a barn for many years. Her adopter placed her in a quiet bedroom of her own, a palatial existence by human standards yet still very strange to her. Her bedroom even offered a beautiful gas fireplace, which emitted a constant hum as the gas fed its fire. What a lucky dog to have a nice bed by a nice fireplace! The poor little dog reacted fearfully each time the warming fire was ignited, and tried to escape the room.

A plug-in insect repellant was also in her room, emitting a sound usually inaudible to humans. But dogs, with their magnificent hearing, are able to hear this sound. This little breeder dog found yet another source of distress, even amongst the luxury of her own, new bedroom. Strange as it may seem to us, this dog would have preferred to be back in her cage, where she was at least familiar with her surroundings.

But fear of loud noises may be due to more than simple lack of exposure to them. Dogs are highly visually-oriented creatures. According to Dr. Temple Grandin, author of *Animals in Translation,* animals see in pictures.[2] Animals capture a great deal of information about their environment by simply watching others. When dogs are trapped like they are trapped in their crates in puppy mills, what they can see is limited. They are denied visual stimulation and may in fact be like a blind animal. But when one sense is almost eliminated, another sense tends to take over. For these dogs, their sense of hearing may become more acute and make them sensitive to loud noises. Dr. Grandin, who is autistic, has found that she and many other autistics cannot tolerate high-pitched sounds. The blare of an alarm, the alerting beep of a truck in reverse, and even the screams of playful children, can all cause distress.

[2]Grandin, T. and Johnson, C. (2005). Animals in Translation: Using the Mysteries of Autism to Decode Animal Behavior. New York, New York: Scribner.

Quick Movements and Loud Noises

Breeder dogs have untrusting natures from experience and so most of them are very skittish. Anyone or anything that moves unexpectedly or suddenly can cause your dog to react in fear. Until your dog becomes more comfortable in its new environment, it will almost always overreact.

But there are many things that you can do to help. Make sure that anyone who interacts with your dog approaches slowly and quietly, with their hands either behind their backs, at their sides or extended in front, where your dog can see them.

If you want to pet your dog, bring your hand up slowly to pet underneath the dog's chin. Show your dog your hand. Allow your dog to sniff your hand, which will help them understand that you are not a threat. At first, do not pet your breeder dog on the head—all dogs consider petting on the head to be a demonstration of domination, which can be threatening and cause fear. Dogs who have been grabbed by the scruff of their neck are also often fearful of hands above their heads.

Breeder dogs are generally not accustomed to the noise of common household appliances like hair dryers and vacuum cleaners. Unless properly introduced, these sounds can frighten the dog to run to his or her safe place or, at worst, try to escape the home and remain phobic in that house from that point on. Do not run such mechanical appliances near your breeder dog for at least the first several days, if not weeks.

Begin slowly and do not expose your dog to too much noise at once. If you regularly use a coffee grinder or blender or hair dryer, make sure that your dog is in another room, or even outside, where the noise will not be so loud. If it still reacts fearfully, act as if nothing unusual is happening (because it isn't) and try to either ignore or distract your dog.

Vacuum cleaners seem to be a source of stress for many dogs, breeder or not. Their unusually loud noise and sweeping movements across the floor can make many dogs fearful. Give your

Quick Movements and Loud Noises
(Continued)

dog at least a week to settle into your home before you attempt to vacuum your house. Use a carpet sweeper or similar alternative in the meantime. When you must vacuum, move your dog to another room or even outside but do not place your dog in a crate: If they become fearful, they might feel trapped and try to escape, and when your dog discovers no means of escape, they may feel like they're back at the breeder's and panic deeply. Allow your dog to find its own safe place for comfort as you move your vacuum from room to room.

Bustery Bustery Boo

Buster has mixed feelings about football season, for sure. He waits in his crate with anticipation when the gang comes over to watch football. "Will I get some pizza crust?" Buster seems to wonder.

But are these few fleeting gulps of that precious crunchy, chewy dough really worth it? Every few minutes, these people jump up and down and scream. Why do they DO that? "These loud, boisterous people," Buster's glance seems to say, "Why can't they be as reserved and quiet as me?"

Born on August 6, 2002, freed from the captivity of a puppy mill on July 20, 2007, and adopted by Chris and Jill Slawecki on September 1, 2007, Buster still shows many emotional scars from the five years he spent confined in his cage. At DVGRR for those three months, Buster was a very withdrawn boy. In typical rescued puppy mill dog fashion, he was difficult to approach and shut down if anyone tried to pet him. He did not run; he simply stopped in place. He clearly did not enjoy human interaction and his body language showed his discomfort as he huddled next to the fence gate—the closest path back to the safety of his kennel.

This was a real shame because "Bustery Bustery Boo" is a big Golden with the huggable looks of a reddish-brown teddy bear and a sad face that can melt even the hardest heart. That's the face that convinced Chris and Jill to bring Buster home, and the face that one year later still brings tears of compassion and pride to their eyes.

Buster's new world at the Slawecki residence was at first a very scary place for him. He did not like to walk on the leash—the first challenge. With his new leash and some coaxing, Chris was able to get Buster to walk around the block within the first few days of adoption. But fate had other plans in store for Buster.

The Slaweckis live within a few blocks of their local high school. Since he was adopted in September, he arrived in his new home during football season. Buster's first Friday night in his new home was also the night of the first home football game at the nearby school. Chris set out for a leisurely stroll with Buster in the cool of a soft September evening and Buster was doing quite well. Suddenly, there was a loud BOOM! Chris jumped and Buster sprawled out on the ground and flattened himself like a pancake, unmoving and unmovable.

"Buster, Buster, get up!" Chris pleaded with him. But Buster was frozen in place, trapped in his terror-filled panic.

Chris bought his maternal grandmother's house which was in the same neighborhood he had lived in his entire life. Cannon fire when the local high school football team scored a touchdown was a simple fact of life in the neighborhood. It was easy for Chris to disregard—until Buster arrived.

Chris eventually convinced Buster to get up and walk back home, and it took several weeks for Chris to be able to coax him back outside for a walk. More than one year later, Buster still likes to retreat to his crate when the sun goes down. One wonders if Buster associates the approaching darkness with those cannon booms.

Take Cover!

It's a good thing that the Slaweckis have a very large fenced-in yard, which is where I visited Buster and where he introduced me to his "sister," FaithBuffy, the Slawecki's female Golden Retriever. Faith (for short) is a peppy, playful, and trusting girl. When a pastor friend of the Slaweckis first met Faith, he called her "the Unfallen Dog," a nickname that Chris loves because Faith really is the way that every dog was created to be—loyal and loving and brimming with life.

When Chris and I watch Buster chase after Faith around their yard, I see such pride in Chris' eyes. Buster did not have much opportunity—or spirit—to run in his former life. His first few attempts, tentative but hopeful if clumsy gallops, led Chris to tell me that Buster runs like he "just discovered that he has legs." These moments of joy and others like them—like Buster's "happy dance" when he now spies Chris grab the leash for their morning walk—have made their journey over the past year worthwhile.

But there were so many moments of doubt. Buster's biggest issues are with noises and sudden movements. Like many puppy mill dogs, Buster is thunder phobic. Just one peal will send Buster to the farthest corner in the back of his crate, and he may not come out for hours. The defining moment for Buster and the Slaweckis was Buster's first thunderstorm in his new home, a storm that began about 1:00pm and lasted until the skies cleared around 6:30 the next morning. Buster simply would not leave his crate for anything during this storm. He huddled in there, his sad and lonely eyes staring back mutely as Chris tried to get Buster out to go to the bathroom. Late that night, concerned that Buster would harm himself by not eliminating for so long, Chris considered returning Buster to DVGRR.

"It's just not working," he sorrowfully confessed to Jill as they climbed the stairs and went to bed, leaving Buster in his crate downstairs with its door wide open.

Chris slept poorly and came downstairs early the next morning, just after the storm had stopped. When he reached the bottom of the stairs, he almost couldn't believe his eyes: Buster had surrounded himself with his soft chew toys and stolen socks and towels, then sprawled out on all fours in the middle of them. When Buster spied Chris, he wagged his tail and looked up as if to say, "I know we had a bad night. Could we maybe start all over this morning? Would you like to share my toys and play?"

Chris could barely see through his tears as his hand reached to turn the knob and open the front door so Faith and Buster could run outside to the yard. When the dogs tumbled out through the doorway and began to romp in the sunny wet grass, Chris began to hope that Buster was ready to accept the love that his family wanted so badly to share with him. He knew that they all needed to press on. For Buster's sake.

Sudden movements and quick hand gestures can still send Buster into a panic, but he recovers much more quickly now. He is also getting accustomed to many new noises, like the neighbor's lawnmower. A noise that most of us think nothing about can be a nightmare for Buster.

Take Cover!

Like white plastic grocery bags, for example, which Chris and his family used to pick up after Faith on their neighborhood walks. When snapped open, they make a distinctive noise. But they soon discovered that snapping these bags open sent Buster into a panic. So the Slaweckis bought smaller, quieter "designer" black bags that made no sound when opened, to clean up after their walks. Buster eventually overcame his fear of white plastic grocery bags!

Dealing with Buster's noise phobia has been challenging, but together they are making strides. More difficult to accept, however, is Buster's tendency to shut down and emotionally withdraw, often for no apparent reason. Chris and Jill and their family all want so very much to love Buster and it can be difficult for them to not take it personally when Buster won't let them into his world. With time, they hope, Buster will open up emotionally. He is most comfortable with Chris and their daughter, Sarah. Their son, Christian, is a big teddy bear (much like Buster) although much more expressive and emotional; Christian's sweeping and often loud movements can be a little scary for Buster. Jill is very loving and accepting of Buster but he seems to remain just a little unsure of her. Recently, Buster bestowed a little kiss on Jill—one more moment of triumph!

Buster continues to learn more every day. Just a few short months ago, he showed interest in playing with a ball. Chris can only toss it a few feet away from Buster, but Buster does bring it back, a few slow feet at a time. For a "normal dog," especially a Golden Retriever, this is no big deal. But for a puppy mill dog who never knew the joys of playing with a ball, this is a huge step!

Although he often seems unsure of how to play, it's for sure that Buster loves to play, and that he has a special interest in toys—destroying them! He likes to rip soft, squeaky toys apart to find their little squeak mechanism, and spreads the stuffing out all over the floor. He's also a bit on the mischievous side and loves to steal socks and soft slippers. His favorite toy remains the little stuffed Froggie which came with him from DVGRR to his new home. Buster frequently searches for it so he can bring it into his crate with him at bedtime.

Buster has made some incredible strides. Even so, he still needs a great deal of coaxing to go into the kitchen and eat his meals. Chris and Jill must leash Buster and lead him through each one of three doorways very slowly to reach their final destination: Food! Is it fear of doorways, dislike of the feel of the linoleum floor, or something else that scares him?

As Chris watches Buster snoozing in his crate, with FaithBuffy near Buster's side, he chokes up a little and admits, "He's so brave to want to trust us."

Take Cover!

Tips to Get Your Dog to Feel Comfortable Around Strangers

♥ Frequently have visitors to your home and invite them to give your dog high value treats. Allow your dog to retreat to his or her safe place if being around people is too stressful.

♥ Take your dog out in public (always on a leash!) to get your dog socialized around people. Do not allow strangers to reach for your dog.

♥ When your dog is ready, enroll in a basic obedience class (positive-rewards only). Look for trainers who understand the special needs of an under-socialized, fearful dog.

Chapter Six

Stacked one on top of the other are rows of small wire cages housing dogs—many, many dogs. Some of the dogs come to the front of their cage to greet me. Others huddle in the back of their cage to get as far away as possible from me...

WHO ARE YOU?

Greeting People

The primary characteristic that runs through all breeder dogs is fear. Most of them want to hide from the world. The reality of existence for dogs like the ones you are meeting in this book is actually much worse and often fraught with more physical abuse than the public will ever know.

Puppy mill breeder dogs really are treated in this manner: Never allowed outside of their cages and producing litter after litter despite sickness, malnutrition, and injury. Very quickly, these dogs learn that escape is impossible, that they are prisoners with no options. When they are no longer able to produce litters, some fortunate dogs are lucky to be freed. Others are left to starve to death or are bludgeoned, shot, or drowned, and killed.

Breeder dogs fortunate enough to be rescued can exhibit strange characteristics quite unlike most "normal dogs." The most consistent of these behaviors occurs if someone approaches them. They go into a panic and often exhibit unusual behaviors such as freezing in place, pacing or spinning, lying flat on the ground, or curling up into a ball. They are attempting to become invisible so you cannot harm them.

Puppy mill breeder dog behavior can resemble autistic human behavior in many ways other than sensitivity to noises. One of the classic signs of autism is a lack of sociability. Autistic children often do not look at other people directly, and generally gaze down or away. We can see this same behavior with rescued puppy mill breeder dogs.

When an under-socialized dog sees a person, the dog is likely to have a flight reaction. The dog is very likely to flee and try to find a place to hide. If access to his or her crate or kennel is available, they will run in there or find another safe corner.

When a person approaches, the dog may curl up into a tight ball to become as small and invisible as possible, or flatten out like a pancake to become one with the floor. These are all desperate attempts to not be seen. Like a child who closes her eyes and says, "You can't see me now," these dogs close their eyes tightly in their attempt to shut out the world. A person is a thing to be feared. We see this reaction in every prey animal who fears their predator in the wild.

Some breeder dogs are likely to fear men more than women, possibly because the breeders who (mis)handled them were men and these dogs associate their cruel treatment more readily with men.

Remy, the Dancing Boy

Just a few months of living in a loving home helped to untuck his fluffy red tail. All it takes now is for someone to say, "Time for a walk," and he wildly thumps that beautiful tail on the floor.

Who Are You?

But Remy's tail was not so fluffy when he met Shelley and Clare McCarthy. He was a very sad boy when he was brought to DVGRR from a Missouri puppy mill in March, 2006. Remy's gait was slow and deliberate, with his head held low. His eyes were as dull as his dirty, matted coat, and he seemed much older than his four years. Those four years of living in a barn unprotected from the elements, with no loving care and poor, cheap food, had taken its toll on not just Remy's health but his spirit, too.

Shelley and Clare came to DVGRR looking to find an active, playful Golden Retriever for their teenage daughter and a friend for their Shih-Tzu, Lizzy. Clare fell in love with one very rambunctious Golden at the April 2006 Adopt-a-Golden Day but when he brought Lizzy over to meet this Golden, the two dogs were clearly incompatible. This Golden lunged and barked at Lizzy.

That's when another Golden caught Clare's eye. He walked up to the sad-faced Remy and he knew immediately that Remy was a diamond in the rough. Shelley was not so sure, but trusted that Clare knew a lot more about what was hidden under that pitiful exterior. When Lizzy met Remy, it was if she agreed with Clare. Remy had found his family.

Remy did not have lots and lots of issues. He was perfectly housetrained, was not afraid of doorways, and from the very beginning walked nicely on the leash. But it was obvious that Remy was never exposed to the good things in life. He did not know how to play with toys, or with other dogs. He clearly had a broken spirit. So Shelley and Clare took it very slowly with Remy. They treated him like a new puppy and were careful not to overload him.

Shelley and Clare slept in the living room with Remy throughout his first night in his new home. He did not like being in the crate, so they decided to restrict his access to the rest of the house; too much too soon would have overwhelmed him. Remy lay quietly on the floor for a few hours, then slowly came over to Shelley and Clare to be petted. The complete trust he gave them was quite a feat for this once unhappy, uncared for dog.

At the start, Remy reserved this trust for only his new family. But Remy's puppy mill personality emerged whenever he saw other people or even other dogs. If someone rang the doorbell, Remy cowered and ran to a safe location, placed his big head between his equally big paws, and hid himself from the world. He was also fearful of loud noises. As a result, Shelley and Clare insisted on new house rules: No doorbells, no hair dryers, and no vacuums, at least until Remy grew more comfortable in his new surroundings.

If they encountered other people or other dogs on their walks, Remy crouched low to the ground and stayed close to his family. Men with deep voices wearing shorts were particularly frightful to Remy, suggesting the obvious conclusion that he was mistreated by such a man at the Missouri puppy mill. Remy's shyness with people is an ongoing work in progress and he is gradually improving.

Who Are You?

Being with Lizzy has helped him a great deal: Lizzy is the leader who walks confidently out front with Remy bringing up the rear. Holding his head low, plodding along as if to say, "I'mmmmmmmmmm oooooo-kkkaaayyy," Remy still walks with his Eeyore-like gait. But don't let that slow walk fool you: If another dog messes with Lizzy, Remy springs into action! One day, they encountered another dog, a German Short-Haired Pointer, who nipped at Lizzy. It didn't take long for Remy to intervene. Remy forgot his fear of other dogs and moved right in between them to protect his little friend.

Their relationship goes both ways. Lizzy was instrumental in getting Remy to come outside into their fenced-in back yard. Remy was very hesitant to go there at first, but now he loves to roll around in the grass and gleefully chases sticks.

The beginning of the relationship between Lizzy and Remy had some difficulties. Remy is quite food motivated; food brings out his true personality and has probably contributed greatly to his progress. Remy was never afraid to eat in front of Shelley and Clare, like many rescued puppy mill dogs. In fact, food brings him to life. He does a dance by shuffling back and forth on his front paws whenever he spies his treats. This Remy-dance is the highlight of daily feeding time. However, his food motivation also created a problem with feeding time. Remy tried to eat Lizzy's food. Although they never fought over food, Shelley and Clare needed to ensure that little Lizzy was able to eat first, which kept Remy from scarfing down Lizzy's food, too.

It wasn't just Lizzy's food that Remy liked. One day, Shelley decided to serve steak for the family's dinner, so she picked out a nice big piece from the freezer and placed it on the kitchen counter to thaw. A couple of hours later, she went into the kitchen and found the wrapper on the floor. "Now, where did that come from?" Shelley wondered. She quickly turned to the counter where she had left their future evening meal and found nothing. No more steak. She did find Remy contentedly napping in the living room, apparently snoozing with a satisfied and full belly. The next time Shelley planned to serve steak for dinner, she figured that she could outwit Remy by placing the steak in the kitchen sink to thaw. He'd never get it from there. Guess what? He did! Talk about a food motivated dog! Steaks now thaw overnight in the McCarthy household refrigerator.

Remy really did need nutrition, which is one reason why he is so food motivated. Even though he weighs a heavy 85 pounds, the muscles in his hind quarters are weak and flabby, possibly due to being crated all of his life, lack of exercise, and partly due to the poor diet at the puppy mill. It's not for lack of exercise in his new home. Shelley and Clare walk him frequently and work with him on playing ball. He did not know what to do with a ball at first, but now he will play fetch once or twice, then lie down as if he's too tired to continue. Anyone who knows Golden Retrievers understands that a four-year-old Golden typically can retrieve for hours, from being bred to serve as hunting dogs, with lots of stamina.

Dogs are not unlike people. Some prefer to be active while others remain couch potatoes. Remy prefers to cuddle, and frequently head butts the nearest person to be petted. Forget the exercise, give me love, Remy seems to say. Remy does have a favorite toy, however. He loves his stuffed donkey from the movie Shrek which says, "Shrek, are we there yet?" when Remy plays with it.

On the cold winter day that I spoke with Shelley and Clare, I asked them if they ever thought about returning Remy to DVGRR because the challenges seemed too great. They both quickly replied, "Never!" Just the thought of how Remy used to spend cold winters in an unheated barn brings tears to their eyes; they are so grateful that Remy has been saved from that life. Shelley has a picture of Remy peacefully lying in the grass as her computer screen-saver at work. She likes to look at him and feel good that she and Clare were able to bring Remy happiness at last.

Reacting to Fearful Behavior

You will experience plenty of times when your breeder dog will show fear. These include going through doorways, up and down steps, during thunderstorms, and no shortage of others!

It is our natural human tendency to feel that if we can somehow manage to give enough love and comfort, everything will be all right. But no amount of love or comfort can change your dog's past. More happily, your demonstrating confident and assured leadership brings much more comfort to your breeder dog. In the past, dog trainers would advise people not to comfort a fearful dog, thinking that the act of comforting may reinforce unwanted fearfulness. Subsequent research and studies now refute this concept.

What to do instead is the question. First and most importantly, try to ignore the behavior or otherwise act as if nothing is wrong or unusual. If your dog sees you acting normally, it may understand that there is no threat and calm down. Or try to distract your dog: Call your dog to come, or call your dog to sit, if your dog responds to these commands. Use your dog's name often, in a happy and upbeat tone, and use food or favorite toys to lure your dog through the situation.

For example, if your dog shows fear of going through a particular doorway, get your dog moving by calling in happy and upbeat tones, and keep on moving right through the doorway, continually calling your dog's name. Do not stop moving—keep moving brightly and confidently and go through the door. If you stop, your dog will think it is okay to stop, too. Keep encouraging, and trying.

From Mom to Lady

Once a month, volunteers with several organizations contact breeders and puppy mills in Lancaster County and ask them if they have any dogs that they no longer want. These volunteers load up several vans with wire dog crates and plastic dog carriers, and generally rescue an average of 30 dogs of all kinds of breeds during these monthly "round ups." They set up a designated meeting place each month, and the dogs are given to various rescue organizations in the area, who take these dogs and either place them in kennels or foster homes until their permanent homes can be found.

In late 2006, a breeder was going to surrender a female Yellow Labrador Retriever to these volunteers, but hesitated because he suspected that she was pregnant. And she was. Soon thereafter, this six-year-old girl had a litter of three puppies. But she wasn't a very good mom. Or maybe she was just tired of being a mom for so many years... or maybe she just wanted out of there...because she stopped nursing her pups. When it became obvious that her breeding days were over, the breeder surrendered her on March 31, 2007.

Through this round-up, this dog met the nice volunteers from Brookline Labrador Retriever Rescue. Brookline is an all-volunteer organization and has no kennel facility so all their dogs go directly into foster homes. This lucky breeder girl found her foster home in West Chester, PA, with Peggy and Mary McGee, sisters who are dedicated to the rescue of Labs. That was the day that she first received her name, and became a Lady.

The McGee's home must be a dog's version of heaven: A large fenced-in yard with a swimming pool and lots and lots of tennis balls. Plus, waiting there with Peggy and Mary were three other dog friends—Gus, Rudy, and Nona—who quickly accepted Lady into their happy Lab pack.

Lady did not exhibit many of the typical traits of scared, rescued breeder dogs the first day that she was there. She was very approachable, ran happily with the other dogs, and barreled right into the house. But then some puppy mill quirks began to surface.

Many breeder dogs are fearful of eating while humans are near. But not Lady: She would NOT eat unless Peggy or Mary was there to hand feed her. Lady had difficulty chewing hard kibble. It was as if she had never eaten hard kibble before, or possibly her teeth and gums hurt. She licked the morsels but then dropped them uneaten onto the floor. Peggy and Mary had to give Lady soft food and gradually mix in the kibble. After about a week or two, Lady was able to eat normally.

Another issue surfaced after that first day: Lady no longer barreled right into the house. She hesitated to come in through the doorway, quite typical for rescued puppy mill dogs. In order to get Lady through the doorway, the other dogs had to go through first, then Lady seemed happy to follow. Rescued puppy mill dogs really need to have other dogs to show them the way.

Housetraining Lady proved to be a relatively minor issue. After a few accidents in the house, Peggy and Mary decided to crate train her. Lady resisted going into the crate, so Peggy and Mary lifted her in. Lady did not freak out when placed into the crate and she seemed calm...or

Who Are You?

so Peggy and Mary thought. One day when they came home from work, Lady had rubbed her nose raw and had been drooling significantly.

That was the last time that Lady was crated. Mary brought Lady into her bedroom and kept her there instead. Lady has never messed her new safe room. But this bedroom also became a place for her to hide—she often wanted to stay in there and refused to come out. When Lady wasn't outside playing with the other dogs, or eating her meals, she preferred the safety of Mary's room.

In the evenings, Peggy and Mary enjoy watching television in their cozy living room but Lady would not come out of the bedroom if the TV was playing in the living room. She peeked her head around the corner tentatively, then bolted back into seclusion when she heard the noises coming from that strange box. Lady even learned that when Peggy picked up the remote control, that fearful noise was about to begin, and she fled when Peggy simply reached into the drawer where the remote control was kept.

Like Dawn with Ginger in chapter three, Peggy and Mary had no intention of adopting Lady at first. They prefer to keep an "open slot" in their home for a foster dog. With Lady, they intended to simply housetrain her, get her accustomed to living in a home, socialize her with people because of her puppy mill background, and then find Lady a good home. But two things quickly derailed these plans: They fell in love with her sweet face, and they started to see her limitations.

Lady is not the perfect specimen, the standard of the Labrador Retriever breed. She has a beautiful blonde coat but her body is long and so are her almost hound dog-like ears. Lady's eyes are her most striking feature, and shine with gratitude and kindness like rays of sunshine on an early spring day. They have a softness that penetrates your soul and warms your heart.

It quickly became obvious that Lady was terrified of strangers. In June 2007, just a couple of months after they had brought her home, Peggy and Mary took Lady to a pet fair where local rescue groups brought their foster dogs in hopes of finding permanent homes for them. Lady sat dutifully by their side as Peggy and Mary handed out leaflets about the Brookline rescue. As people saw Lady and reached to pet her, they commented that she was so calm. But Lady was not calm— she was terrified. She stood frozen in place and could barely tolerate the strangers' advances, no matter how friendly. As she hid behind the metal folding chair as far away from the people as possible, it became obvious to Peggy and Mary that Lady was terrified and was not the social dog that she was at home.

Peggy and Mary decided to take Lady out in public as much as possible to expose her to people and get her more comfortable around strangers. PetSmart® seemed like the perfect place to take Lady—lots of pets and pet lovers and a place to buy tasty treats and happy toys. What more could a dog ask? Lady has no problem with car rides; in fact, she enjoys them. When they arrived at PetSmart®, Lady jumped out of the car, tail wagging in anticipation of their field trip. But when they approached the store, Lady did a quick about-face and pulled hard on her leash to get back into the car. Unwilling to stress Lady, Peggy and Mary did not force her to go into the store. After this adventure, Lady does not go out much.

Lady's reaction to trips away from home notwithstanding, she still needed to become more comfortable around strangers or else she would be very difficult to place in her permanent home. Peggy and Mary like to welcome visitors to their home, and Lady needed to become accustomed to seeing unfamiliar faces. But every time that someone would visit Peggy or Mary, Lady retreated to Mary's bedroom. Eventually, the time came when Peggy and Mary decided that Lady needed to face this fear. When visitors arrived, they kept Lady on the leash with them in the living room. Although she wanted to flee, Lady eventually laid down and accepted the presence of strangers.

This same approach helped Lady overcome her fear of the television. At first, Mary held Lady on the sofa while the TV played. With time, Lady grew accustomed to its strange sounds and eventually relaxed in the living room with Peggy and Mary. Now, Lady even claims her own TV-watching spot on the sofa!

There was one exception to Lady's acceptance of the TV: When Peggy and Mary watched *Uncaged*, the documentary about breeder dogs that I co-produced, Lady could hear the sound of barking puppy mill dogs. She bolted from their living room back into Mary's bedroom like she did many months before. Is it possible that Lady had a flashback to her days in the puppy mill? It certainly appeared that way.

Lady's nervousness around strangers and difficulty in going places helped Peggy and Mary realize that it was going to be tough to find a permanent home for her. Most people simply do not understand the challenges of living with a dog with these issues or how to deal with them. Peggy and Mary also did not want Lady to have to go through another period of adjustment in her new home, like she had been through for several months with them. So on September 5, 2007, Peggy and Mary officially adopted Lady as their own. Nona, Gus, and Rudy had a new sister.

But Lady's story does not end with her happy adoption. One day, Peggy and Mary were looking through her paperwork and discovered in a folder a notation that Lady's birthday was September 11, 2001—that day the world will never forget. Even though that was a horrific day for so many, it was also a day that brought Lady into the world and her first step toward Peggy and Mary and their lifetime of love.

Today, Lady's nickname is Ladybug or just Bug for short. She plays with toys and also knows several words, such as "ball," "outside," "sit," "wait," and "paw."

Living with Another Dog

Most breeder dogs have lived with other dogs, often lots of them. Very often, the only time some dogs feel comfortable is in the presence of other dogs. Watch a frightened dog when a person approaches and that dog will run to the closest dog, often hiding behind it. But then watch that same frightened dog when no people are around, and it will often run and play "like a normal dog."

Companion dogs serve two purposes for rescued breeder dogs: They provide a faithful friendship and comfort zone, and are important helpers in the learning process. A scared, uncertain dog needs a guide. Dogs who have never had the opportunity to live in a home with humans can learn so much from being paired with a "normal" dog or even a breeder dog who is a little bolder.

Dogs watch each other very carefully. They get a safe feeling from having a companion who speaks their language. A "normal" dog can teach a frightened dog that life is no longer terrifying. Seeing their companion step out to have some fun makes it easier for your breeder dog to step out and have fun, too.

Molly, Small Yet Mighty

In July 2008, I watch a diminutive black figure, barely taller than the blades of grass, sprint through an expansive back yard. Molly weighed just five pounds when she arrived at her new home that previous February; she's now a healthy eight pounds. Her short legs move at twice the speed of Bentley's and Bitsy's, the two Bull Terriers that Molly lives with, as she tries to keep up with them. Bentley and Bitsy often forget that she's underfoot and Molly goes tumbling down the hill, only to jump up and resume her chase with typical terrier determination. That's the Jack Russell in her.

Bentley and Bitsy hear a dog barking in the yard up the hill and off they run to the split rail fence with Molly hurrying behind as if to say, "Wait for me!," but completely unaware of why everyone is running! She then takes off in a mad dash around the yard like a baseball player rounding the bases, and leaps up onto the deck in a flourish. Molly is safe at home. Truly safe, and truly home.

It's so difficult to imagine that this little sprite was caged in a puppy mill as a breeder dog. But public demand for "designer dogs," otherwise known as <u>very</u> expensive mutts, created this little dog named Molly. She is called a Jug, bred from a Jack Russell Terrier and a Pug, solid black with a Jack Russell's body and head but with the shorter face of a Pug. Her cuteness is irresistible, a blessing accompanied by a curse—the demand for designer Jugs.

What's even more difficult to imagine is that the breeder used her to breed puppies. Molly is deaf—truly a symbol of the greed of puppy millers. No responsible breeder would breed a deaf dog and chance that her deafness would be genetically passed on to her puppies. Molly's sister is also deaf and remains at this puppy mill breeding puppies, her fate unknown but most likely very bleak. Who knows if their puppies are deaf or where people have bought them, likely spending up to $2000 at a pet store or over the internet for that "designer dog" which they simply could not live without.

Molly was not a good mom, which was her salvation. She bred a litter of puppies, and ate them. It's sad but sometimes a fact of life; maybe Molly was starving and thought this was her only hope for survival. The puppy mill owner decided to get rid of her because she was no longer profitable for him. This life-saving incident brought Molly to Main Line Animal Rescue (MLAR), where she met MLAR volunteers Livvy Roth and Donna Iannucci.

Molly found her new MLAR environment to be very stressful, and could not settle down in her new refuge. No matter how terrible the puppy mill was, at least it was familiar. MLAR's spacious new building, which houses over 100 dogs with kennel runs and crates, was unfamiliar to Molly. She barked all night, which kept the other residents awake and barking all night too. She was also losing weight. The veterinarian who examined Molly said that, "she has a failure to thrive."

Molly was also a cage spinner, with an anxiety-related obsessive-compulsive disorder (OCD) that can cause dogs to spin in circles repetitively. Such spinning or pacing is a common OCD with puppy mill dogs who have been confined in small spaces: In an attempt to relieve the anxiety they are feeling from constant confinement, these dogs stay in constant motion. Even released from their cages, they can still continue to spin or pace. This is why Molly was losing weight.

Over the course of several months in late 2007, Molly was in and out of several foster homes but came back to MLAR each time due to housetraining problems and her extreme lack of trust with people. Her stubby little Jack Russell-like tail stayed tucked and never wagged. She ran and hid from everyone. Even some people at MLAR began to suggest that Molly should be euthanized because she seemed so unhappy and was not "thriving."

When Molly came home to Livvy, Donna, Bentley, and Bitsy, the dogs immediately connected. Their house in Coatesville, PA, is large, especially for a tiny girl like Molly, with an even more spacious back yard. The large yard is wide open and grassy on a sloping hill, bordered by a split-rail and wire fence. Reluctantly, Molly stepped out into the openness of freedom and ran with the other dogs by her side.

Communicating with Molly was not easy since she could not hear; combined with her distrust of people, it made living with Molly quite a challenge. Housetraining was, and continues to be, Molly's greatest challenge. Molly offers no signals that she needs to go outside, and it is impossible to ask her if she wants to go out. Consequently, Molly must be treated like she is a puppy. She is on a regular potty schedule and when she cannot be watched, Molly is either in her crate or confined to a small area.

Crates pose their own problem because Molly becomes very anxious when left alone in one: She defecates in the crate, flings it out onto the surrounding walls and floor, and then proceeds to grind the feces into the crate bottom while hysterically jumping to get out. Livvy and Donna faced this messy greeting when they came home each day! (This issue is one reason why I continue to say that people who adopt or foster puppy mill survivors are very special people.)

Luckily, both Livvy and Donna have flexible work schedules and can frequently work at home. But they still needed an alternative to the crate for Molly for days when they could not be home. Livvy and Donna found a large dog care facility and sent Molly there for a few hours to try it out. Doggie daycare to the rescue—Molly loved it! In fact, going to doggie daycare may have helped Molly become more socialized with people. She is welcomed there with open arms, and is very reluctant to leave at the end of the day.

But at home, Molly continued to be tentative with people. She decided that she liked sleeping in Donna's room; the first thing she sees when she awakes each morning is Donna, which has helped Molly become more attached to her. She then began to follow Donna from room to room. Although more comfortable with Donna, Molly still seemed a little afraid of Livvy. Livvy needed to keep Molly on her leash at all times, to make sure that she could catch her.

Molly still runs from everyone and is very fearful of being picked up. Hands are not a good thing in Molly's mind. She remains this cautious still.

After living with Molly for a few weeks, Livvy called on me to provide some guidance. It was difficult for her and Donna to gain Molly's trust. In addition to needing advice to help with housetraining, Molly was difficult to get close to. We discussed the basics of housetraining and then quickly moved on to Molly's fear of people. Because Molly is so hand-phobic, we decided that she needed to begin to associate good things coming from hands—especially coming from Livvy's and Donna's hands.

We sat on the floor. Our hands held tempting pieces of canned chicken, and we extended our hands to Molly. Although very tentative, Molly just couldn't resist that enticing smell and her desire for food overrode her fear. But only for a very short time: She curiously approached, smelled, gave a quick lick, and then retreated just as quickly. Like most other rescued puppy mill dogs, Molly needed time and patience so that she could learn to trust on her own terms. Forcing her to accept touch could cause more fear and even biting. Smaller puppy mill dogs, especially terriers, have a tendency to bite when placed in a cornered or fearful position.

I coached Livvy and Donna to not grab for Molly as they gave her the chicken, to just allow her to come on her own without the fear of being grabbed, so she could begin to trust them. So Livvy and Donna decided to coat their hands with Molly's canned food every day, to help Molly feel more at ease with them. How could Molly resist?

Who Are You?

Just how does one communicate with a deaf dog? Livvy and Donna learned quickly that Molly picked up on hand signals. Every time that Molly did something right, Livvy and Donna gave her the "thumbs-up" sign with a great big smile. They needed to proceed cautiously, of course, with any hand movement, to avoid scaring her. But a slow motion without reaching toward Molly did the trick. Every time that Molly went to the door to signal that she needed to go outside, they gave her the thumbs-up. Every time that Molly eliminated in the yard, she got two thumbs-up!

"Do you use a hand signal to tell her to go potty?" I asked.

"We use a circular motion," Livvy explained as she swept her hand around in the air.

Molly has progressed to the point that her tail wags and she happily greets Donna when Donna comes home from work. Lots of kisses are showered on Donna, and vice versa! Molly remains a little more cautious around Livvy, possibly because Molly sleeps with (often lying on top of) Donna. When Donna is not home, Molly will follow Livvy around the house and will watch her closely. But she can still flee, and if she does, she can be difficult to catch.

When I arrived to interview Donna and Livvy for this book, I was stunned to see Molly come to the door and greet me. In just a few short months she has gained the confidence to approach people. However, she still ran from me when I tried to slowly reach for her. She ran to her safe corner in the hallway and hid. Of course, I came prepared and brought out the secret weapon—chicken. Within about half an hour,

Molly ventured out to see me. I couldn't believe it when I felt a tiny little lick on my hand as Molly came close to me. I didn't even have the chicken in my hand when she did it!

It's very sad for me that I cannot pet Molly and give her a little hug like I want to pet and hug all dogs, to show her the affection she deserves. Molly's so cute and irresistible that it's tough to squelch that urge in respect of her own needs. But I know that if I try to pet Molly it would only frighten her.

As with most rescued puppy mill dogs, time heals most of the emotional scars but some may remain. It did not matter to Livvy and Donna. In June 2008, they gave me the wonderful news that they had adopted Molly. Donna told me that she knew after just a week or two that Molly was going to stay with them. It took Livvy a little longer to be sure. They're both sure now.

Molly is now a traveling girl. She has flown on an airplane twice and is scheduled to go again. She easily goes into her crate and quietly stays there. She also likes to go shopping—you might find Molly in Livvy's or Donna's purse as they browse through Home Depot® or other unsuspecting stores. Molly also comes back to visit with her friends at MLAR every week, when Livvy volunteers there on Saturdays. Everyone comments on how she has changed. Molly is thriving now.

Molly still has anxiety issues and remains on medication to help her. She takes Prozac to help with her OCD spinning and will be weaning off of the Xanax that helped her acclimate to living in a home and accept the advances of people. Like many rescued breeder dogs, Molly remains hyper-vigilant—her prey animal instinct—so that she can flee quickly when someone approaches. But this acute awareness is also an attribute of deaf dogs. With the loss of one sense, other senses become stronger.

After six months with Livvy and Donna, Molly's tail is really wagging! She's playing with toys, too, and especially loves the big Nylabones that belong to Bentley and Bitsy. She's part terrier, after all, and thinks that she's one of the big dogs! She takes these bones right out of their mouths, and they let her.

Livvy and Donna call Molly a "tough little thing," and she truly is.

Buddy

Buddy

Maggie

Buster

Buster & Faith

Remy & Lizzy

Lady

Lady

Molly

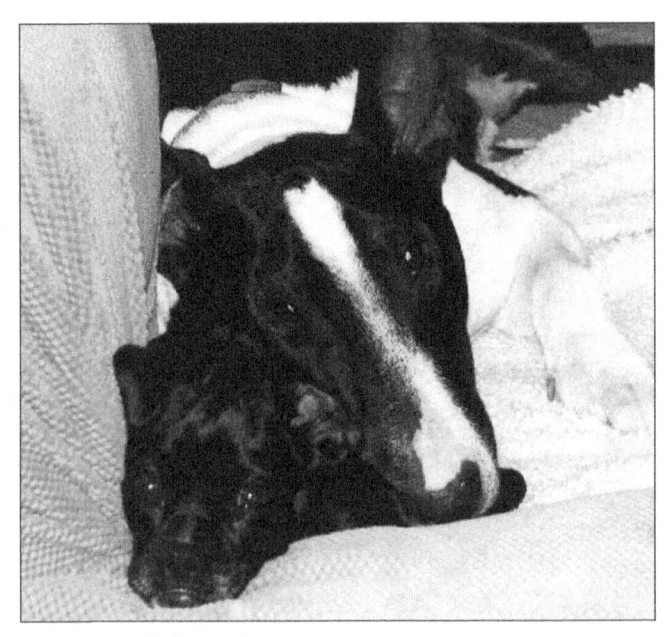

Molly & Big Brother Bentley

Penny

Spin

Oscar

Oscar

Who Are You?

Tips for Getting Your Dog to Trust Your Hands

♥ Sit on the floor or the ground with your hand extended out to the side while holding some high value treats. Try not to make eye contact with your dog.

♥ Allow your dog to come over to you without coaxing it verbally.

♥ If your dog approaches you, do not reach for your dog, even to pet it. And make no sudden moves or vocalizations that might scare your dog. Just allow your dog to take the treats.

♥ Hand-feed your dog's meals. Sit on the floor and feed your dog out of its bowl several nuggets at a time.

♥ Avoid any swift hand movements.

♥ Discourage anyone from trying to pet your dog on the head. This is a threatening gesture.

Chapter Seven

Most cages contain several dogs, lying on top of one another. I realize that one of the smells that greeted me when I entered the barn was dog waste.

HANDS ARE GOOD THINGS

Being Touched

Sadly, breeder dogs may have been rarely handled by humans and only for the most negative purposes and circumstances: The breeder may have needed to move the dog out of the cage and painfully grabbed the dog by the scruff of the neck or one of his or her legs. Many breeder dogs may have only been handled by humans when it was time for them to breed or when their puppies were taken from them.

This fear is often worse for females than for their male counterparts because they associate human touch with the invasiveness of the breeding process. Lily, who we met in chapter four, for example, immediately sits down when she sees a person and cringes if anyone approaches her from the rear. She is afraid of the invasive breeding process. Lily is essentially a canine rape victim.

These dogs most likely never enjoyed the pleasure of being gently petted by someone who loves them. They never had the opportunity to associate pleasure with humans.

After being mistreated in these ways, these dogs become like prey animals who flee at the sight of a threat. There are varying extremes:

Some dogs seem to have the resiliency to endure and suffer abuse and yet still know that humans can also give love and affection. Other dogs have personalities that make them run in fear.

Dogs like this have learned that they have no options for escape; the only reaction they have left is to turn themselves off. The psychological term for this is "learned helplessness." Prisoners of war often exhibit learned helplessness. So do people who have been kidnapped, and people trapped in any kind of abusive situation, such as victims of domestic violence.

What, exactly, is learned helplessness? By definition, it's a psychological condition where humans or animals have learned that they have no options to escape their mentally and physically painful situation, and have no control over their environment. The victims feel that whatever they do is futile. As a result, they will stay passive in an unpleasant or harmful situation, based on the assumption that escape is impossible.

The theory of learned helplessness was developed in 1965 by Dr. Martin Seligman at the University of Pennsylvania through experiments aimed at discovering more about depression in humans.[3] In these controlled experiments, dogs were conditioned to associate hearing a sound with receiving an electric shock. Dogs were strapped into harnesses, heard the sound, then were administered the shock. The first dog was only put into the harness for a period of time and then released. The second dog was put in the harness and received electric shocks, which the dog could stop

---

[3]Seligman, M.E.P., Maier, S.F., and Geer, J. (1968). "The alleviation of learned helplessness in dogs." Journal of Abnormal Psychology, 73, 256-262.

by pressing a lever when he heard the sound. The third dog was wired in parallel with the second dog and received shocks of equal intensity and duration, but, when pressed, his lever did not stop the shocks.

The first and second dogs quickly recovered from the experience. But the third dog learned that he was helpless no matter what he did. He consequently suffered chronic symptoms of clinical depression.

A slightly different experiment was conducted on two groups of dogs placed in hammocks. The first group was given shocks but was able to make the shocks stop; the second group was given shocks they were unable to stop. Later, they were put in a room that was divided in half by a low barrier. The first group of dogs saw a flash of light ten seconds before they received a shock, enough time for them to jump over the barrier to escape the shock. The second group also saw the light ten seconds before being shocked, but because they had "learned helplessness" from the previous experiment, they just lay down and whined. Even though they could have escaped being shocked, they did not even attempt to try.

The behaviors of breeder dogs who have suffered at the hands of puppy mill owners directly and consistently imitate the behaviors of the dogs in these 1965 experiments.

The Lucky Penny

Ann, who had only lived with "normal dogs" all her life, adopted one such fearful dog: Penny, a breeder dog rescued from a Lancaster County farm. In the fall of 2005, DVGRR obtained the scared little dog from the farm and named her Stella. At that time, DVGRR and other rescue groups had very little experience with breeder dogs and their often odd behavior. These dogs were simply deemed to be "shy." No one realized the issues these dogs could present when they went to live in homes.

Ann had recently lost another Golden at age ten, and adopted Stella to be a companion for her seven-year-old Golden Retriever, Breeze. Breeze needed a new friend. When Ann met Stella, Stella ran from her but Ann's heart went out to her. Ann felt that she could help, but she had no idea about the long road she and Stella were about to venture down together. This was the beginning of an incredible journey that Ann could never have imagined and would change her life.

Stella was unmanageable from the very moment she came into Ann's home. Stella could not relax; she paced for hours. Ann left open the door to the fenced backyard so that Stella could come and go as she pleased; Stella would not re-enter the house unless Ann was completely out of sight. Then Stella ran from Ann and would not let her come near her. Ann had always been a little timid around dogs and did not want to force Stella to interact with her.

Another problem quickly became evident: Stella was not housetrained. Ann was told that Stella had no accidents in the kennel at DVGRR but this certainly changed once she came home. Ann had also purchased a crate for Stella, thinking that it might provide her with a "safe place," but Stella wanted nothing to do with it. Placing treats and even Stella's meals in the crate could not entice her to enter it.

Hands Are Good Things

Ann's first few days of life with Stella were torture. Ann could not sleep. The reward for her kindness was having her life controlled by a very frightened dog who would not even stay in the same room with her. Ann's frustration and stress were peaking after four days of not being able to touch, confine, or leash Stella. She contacted a veterinary behaviorist for advice but he could not give her an appointment for at least a month. He also told her that Stella would require months of therapy and medication to rehabilitate her.

It all seemed to pile up on her at once and a frustrated Ann decided to return Stella to DVGRR.

And Ann would have driven Stella back to DVGRR herself except for one problem—she couldn't even get Stella on a leash to get her in the car! How could Ann take Stella back if she couldn't even capture her?

So Ann arranged for a DVGRR volunteer to come to her house. The volunteer finally managed to loop a leash around Stella's neck and asked Ann, "Do you still want to return Stella?"

As Ann later put it: "If I could have gotten her on a leash, I would have taken her back. But if I could have gotten her on a leash, there would have been no need to take her back." Once that leash was on, Ann decided that she would keep Stella.

Stella had one more bad habit when she became more comfortable in Ann's house. She liked to chew, especially when Ann was not home. Her favorite things to chew were books. Ann came home from work one day to find an old book in shreds on the living room floor, a book titled

The Penny Puppy. Ann never really cared for the name "Stella" so she took this as a sign that her funny little dog's name had to be Penny.

Ann has always been a little afraid of dogs. Because of her timidity around dogs, Ann was not willing to corner Penny. She didn't want Penny to become so fearful that she might bite, even though Penny never once showed any indication that she would. Penny may also have sensed Ann's own trepidation. For almost the first eight months, Ann was not able to touch Penny. Finally, Ann was able to lightly touch the side of Penny's face but only for a few fleeting seconds. Nevertheless, it was an exciting moment! Things slowly kept getting better every day. Ann was comfortable with their arrangement, and felt certain that Penny's life was 100% better than it had been in the puppy mill.

Every morning and night, Ann patiently fed Penny her meals by hand. Ann sat in a chair in her living room with one hand outstretched so that Penny could creep into the room and take small nibbles of food. Ann took great pains not to look at Penny because any eye contact made Penny flee. Penny inched forward one slow step at a time, ate a little, and ran away. As a result, mealtime usually lasted about half an hour. (Now, that's dedication!) This exercise was so important in building the bond of trust with Penny that Ann still continues to hand-feed Penny her dinner every night. Dinner is their special bonding time, and it cements their relationship more and more.

Each day, Penny watched as Ann took Breeze for her daily walk. Penny could not join them on their walks because Penny would not

Hands Are Good Things

allow Ann to touch her. Then, one magical summer day, Ann felt Penny come up next to her as she was putting the leash and harness on Breeze. Ann could hardly contain her happiness when Penny stood patiently while Ann put the harness on her! Knowing this was a tremendous accomplishment for Penny, Ann still could not resist giving Penny a little pat. Penny was more receptive to being touched from that day on, a little at a time and usually while wearing her harness.

Penny could happily go for walks, but some issues remained. Penny did not like to go out without Breeze. Breeze gave her confidence and she liked having her friend with her. Penny is also a creature of habit. Ann cannot change the direction of their walks without Penny freezing in place. Much like an obsessive-compulsive person, Penny needs a certain, specific routine and becomes unsettled if there are any changes. Penny has stopped in the middle of the street and Ann can only get her to move with a lot of verbal coaxing (and cheese). Ann will not walk Penny at night because of this issue—it's just too risky. However, getting Penny to walk again after she stopped in the street also provides Ann with moments of triumph. Early in their relationship, Penny simply would not move.

Soon after their first walk together, Penny allowed more petting from Ann. Penny liked being close to Ann and followed her around the house, but would run if Ann tried to pet her. Penny also claimed Ann's bed from almost the very beginning and slept with her all night, but if Ann tried to pet her, Penny jumped off the bed. Imagine Ann's frustration from all those months of not being able to touch her own dog! But all of this gradually changed. Ann can now sit on the sofa next to Penny and Penny enjoys her petting time. She even likes to be brushed!

Outside, Penny is very territorial and appears to be a "normal dog." She barks when people walk past her yard. She is especially curious when she sees children, although she shies away when they attempt to pet her. She loves to be outside except for one mysterious source of trouble: Penny is very fearful of hoses and watering cans. She runs inside when Ann waters her plants. Her reaction makes me think that her fear is a result of living in a barn that was occasionally washed down by some type of water source. Was it a hose or a bucket? Was Penny sprayed in the face by accident? On purpose? Who can tell? It is one more peculiarity in a dog caused by being raised under such cruel conditions. Because of this issue, Ann cannot get Penny anywhere near the bathroom to give her a bath. Luckily, Penny is a naturally clean dog!

One thing still concerns Ann. Penny will only allow Ann and two of Ann's friends to pet her. No one else can even come near her, at least not yet. If Ann needed to leave Penny overnight or longer, she has a very limited number of people who could care for Penny. Sending Penny to a kennel would be out of the question. Even the chance that Penny may regress must be avoided at all costs!

To help Penny overcome her social anxiety, Ann enrolled both Penny and Breeze in a class designed to increase the dogs' confidence; even though Breeze had plenty of confidence already, she attended with

Penny because Penny did not like to go anywhere without her. This Confidence Class used several different techniques to help under-socialized and fearful dogs. Each class began with touching exercises to help relax the dog. A brief massage and head-to-tail stroking was needed to calm the dogs because there were several other dogs and people in the classroom. Other exercises included changing handlers, walking through obstacles, and using agility equipment. For a dog like Penny, changing handlers was quite a challenge. Yet she allowed a total stranger to take her leash and walk around the room with her.

Penny deserves so much praise for reaching beyond her fears and learning to trust Ann. Ann also deserves praise for not giving up on Penny. But we must recognize Breeze's contribution as well: Penny carefully examined Ann's interactions with Breeze. She saw Breeze getting lots of love and attention, and noticed Breeze's happy reaction. Ann believes that Penny learned to trust Ann and come forward for affection because Breeze gave Ann credibility in Penny's eyes. It must have looked to Penny like she was missing something really good! Breeze acted in very much the same capacity as a service dog helps a special needs person. Penny did not like to go anywhere without her. Breeze showed Penny how to be a dog and led the way for her.

Breeze also acted as Penny's playmate. Penny's true dog personality emerged during their playtime. Penny played rather roughly with Breeze, and Ann needed to be vigilant of their interactions. Breeze occasionally wearied of Penny's persistence and needed time away from

Penny. In her defense, Penny was emotionally a puppy—she was never allowed to play when she really was a puppy. She's making up for lost time. Sometimes much to Breeze's dismay!

Sadly, Breeze developed cancer in the fall of 2007 and quickly passed away. But several months before then, Ann adopted Spin, another puppy mill dog from DVGRR. I'll tell his story in our next chapter.

Living with Penny and her challenges certainly changed Ann's lifestyle to better accommodate Penny's needs. But there's more: After taking film-making classes for several years, Ann filmed a documentary on the lives of rescued breeder Golden Retrievers transitioning from puppy mills to happy homes—*Uncaged, Second Chances for Puppy Mill Breeder Dogs*. *Uncaged* has been shown on public television and many other venues since March 2008. Without Penny, this film would never have been conceived. Ann hopes that the public will be able to witness through this film the atrocities inflicted upon our beloved dogs and to effect changes for the better.

The process has been very rewarding and endearing, according to Ann. Almost three years later, Penny enjoys her walks and especially likes to visit with Ann's friend Maureen. Maureen also has a Golden Retriever, Seamus, plus a nice big yard. Penny, Seamus, and now Spin, all love to play together, and Penny becomes like a puppy as she scoots around the yard. Penny and the other dogs also get lots of tasty snacks that add to their fun.

Hands Are Good Things

Penny has her silly side. The dog who used to be so timid and nervous now likes to steal Ann's pajamas from beneath her pillow and drag them into the living room. Now nothing is off limits—shoes, other clothing, and, of course, books. Penny's favorite things, however, are her stuffed snowman and reindeer. She prances around the yard with one of them in her mouth, has been known to bury them in the yard, and sometimes Ann finds them buried among the cushions of her living room couch.

Despite her tremendous improvements, Penny can still be spooked. One day during their walk, a man approached them on the sidewalk. Normally, Penny would not stop. But this time, the man stumbled and his flip-flop made a slapping noise on the ground.

"I'm sorry!" he said as he reached to comfort Penny. But Penny backed up and moved away from this apologetic man. Despite these little setbacks, Ann says, "What a stretch it is now for Penny to trust an outstretched hand."

Body Work

Science recognizes the need for animals, including humans, to be touched, and the value of massage. The sensation of being massaged creates electrical impulses that feel calming to the body. Massage can relieve stress and lower blood pressure. Deep tissue massage relaxes the body and releases toxins that can collect in muscle tissue and cause discomfort.

Touch and massage also lowers the production and accumulation of the stress hormones cortisol, epinephrine and norepinephrine. This is especially important for many breeder dogs, who practically live in a constant state of fear and produce these stress hormones all the time.

Many breeder dogs have been handled very roughly and can associate hands with rough treatment. For example, the breeder may have used food in one hand to lure the dog to them, then grabbed the dog with their other hand when the dog approached. Keeping your hand movements slow and gentle is vital.

Start by touching your dog's ears. Dogs have more sense receptors at the tips of their ears and at the front of their ear canal. Keep your touch light and slow. Slowly bring your hand up underneath your dog's chin and lightly touch your dog's ear. If your dog does not try to move away, continue to touch the ear, rubbing the tip between your thumb and forefinger. Watch for any sign of discomfort and discontinue if your dog begins to show stress. If your dog seems to be enjoying it, move your fingers up and down the ear. Lightly massage the indentation in the front of your dog's ear with your forefinger. This is an acupressure point that produces relaxation. Constantly talk softly, praising your dog, while you are massaging.

Limit your first ear massage session to just a few minutes. You can gradually work up to longer sessions and to other parts of the body. If your dog shows fear at any time, discontinue the session and ignore the fear. If your dog does not run from your touch and seems to like it, extend the massage to other body parts.

It helps to give your dog a short massage before you take your dog into circumstances that may cause stress.

Hands Are Good Things

Tips for Crate Training

- Place the crate in a room that you and your dog frequently occupy but in a safe, out-of the way corner.

- Gradually introduce your dog to the crate by keeping the door open and accessible to your dog.

- Place high value treats in the crate and allow your dog to retrieve them without shutting the door.

- Once your dog is freely entering the crate, begin the process of closing the door. Again, feed high value treats as you close the door, leaving it closed for only a few seconds. Praise your dog and open the door.

- Continue practicing until your dog is comfortable with the crate door closed.

- Never place your dog in the crate as a punishment. It must have only positive associations.

Chapter Eight

The caged dogs were eliminating right in their cages. When these wastes piled up in the dog cages on the top of these stacks, it overflowed onto the dogs in the bottom cages...

I'M NEVER GOING BACK IN A CAGE AGAIN

Crate Training—Yes or No?

Crates are popular for teaching a dog housetraining manners. Dogs like the security of a confined space. They look to find a location to rest where their backs are protected from the possibility of something sneaking up on them. Take some time to watch dogs when they wish to rest: They search out spots that give them protection—under the bed, behind the sofa, in a corner of the kitchen, under a tree or a deck. The crate mimics a dog's den in the wild.

A dog will not eliminate in their den. Dogs know to eliminate in places away from their den because the smell attracts predators. Using a cage or crate to housetrain a dog mimics a dog's natural instinct to find a den.

Breeder dogs, however, never had that luxury. Breeder dogs were always confined to their crates. Consequently, using a crate to housetrain and give a rescued breeder dog a safe place to sleep may not be a viable option for you. You will know fairly quickly if your dog becomes very upset when placed into their crate. Yet other dogs run into their crate for safety. While the crate may be a safe haven for some of these dogs, others may feel like it is their jail. It depends on each individual dog, and his or her temperament and experiences.

Spin—A Glow From Within

During their daily walk, Ann Metcalf smiles as Spin approaches cars stopped for the red light near their house. Spin looks at the passengers and happily wags his tail. Many people comment, "What a beautiful dog!"

Why does this make Ann smile? Because Spin is not your typical-looking Golden Retriever. He's smaller than normal, slender, and has a small, slightly crooked face, far from the block-headed Goldens you see in competitive dog shows. But what people can immediately see is not what people admire about Spin. It's his beauty radiating out from within. Spin is one of the happiest dogs that I have ever met, with soulfully soft and kind eyes. Spin had a starring role in the film *Uncaged*. But his previous years were not so stellar.

Spin was surrendered to the Humane League of Lancaster in January, 2007. His paperwork stated "evidence hold" for apparent cruelty to animals. Less than one week later, Spin was brought to DVGRR. He was small for a Golden, with weepy eyes, a crooked face, and a muzzle that looked like it had gotten in the way of a mad horse's hoof. His blonde fur was patchy, brittle, and dry, not soft and silky like most Goldens'.

This boy, a little shy and aloof, was the most nervous and anxious breeder dog I had seen to date. DVGRR hosted five other rescued

I'm Never Going Back in a Cage Again

breeder dogs at the time—all females—and none of them even came close to the anxiety that Spin exhibited. In his kennel, he spun frantically in circles whenever anyone walked by, which is how he got his name—the staff named him Spinner. If you approached him, he jumped up and bit at the latch (in between spinning), as if desperately trying to say, "Let me out!"

Once out of the kennel, Spinner was a happy guy. He quickly became very trusting and friendly. He jumped on people with the gentle touch of the tiniest flea, to ask for a hug. In return, his sparse tail wagged happily in appreciation. Although his tail communicated his pleasure, his frowning brow conveyed the worried look of a dog who had not been treated lovingly over the past seven years. He demonstrated the characteristic slinking behavior of most breeder dogs when approached, or when they hear a noise. Cautiously, and literally, they hit the ground.

Spinner stayed at DVGRR for three months to recover and heal both physically and emotionally (that's the beauty of DVGRR—it's like a "halfway house" where dogs can come to recover and prepare to move on to their "forever home"). But Spinner wasn't making any emotional progress. His kennel spinning continued. He was unable to gain weight despite being fed and eating lots of calorie-dense food three times a day. I recommended putting Spinner on anti-anxiety medication in hopes it would stop his spinning, but before he received any medication, he found an adopted home! A very nice man and woman fell in love with Spinner's gentle face and friendly demeanor. They also adopted another Golden Retriever that same day so that the dogs could keep each other company.

Spinner was nervous in his new home but he was no longer spinning in circles. Noises startled him, and steps were scary. He preferred to be outside on the deck. But he was frightened even there because the hot tub motor routinely cycled on and off. His adopters loved him very much right from the beginning, but they did not realize how much of a "project" it would be to help Spinner adjust to living in a loving family home.

Spinner left urine accidents on his fleece bed and bowel movements near his food dish in the living room. Then Spinner tracked them around the house. Even though he was seven years old, Spinner was like a new puppy, and required constant attention to housetrain.

Even after all of this, Spinner's new owners were reluctant to crate him because they knew of his bad experiences. Eventually, they decided to barricade him in the kitchen at night, with their other dog. They blocked the kitchen entrance with an expandable baby gate, and braced a wooden dining room chair against the gate to keep it from falling.

The defining moment occurred one night about ten days after Spinner had been adopted. Spinner did not want to stay in the kitchen that night. He barked for quite a while. His adopters heard a loud bang and then a yelp! They rushed to the kitchen; there they found Spinner, lying on the floor with his head stuck through the slats of the chair. Frantically, they removed the chair and checked him for injuries. Thankfully, he was unhurt. Then Spinner made a dash for the deck!

I'm Never Going Back in a Cage Again

All of these things helped Spinner's adopters realize that they had taken on more than they could handle. They tearfully drove Spinner back to DVGRR while he slept comfortably in their back seat. His spinning in the kennel resumed.

When Ann Metcalf heard this news, she felt awful for the poor guy and considered fostering Spinner. After all, she had adopted Penny, another breeder dog, about one and a half years before, and she knew that she could handle house training Spinner. As Ann was filming footage for *Uncaged*, our documentary about rescued breeder dogs and their quests for lives in loving families, one late May day at DVGRR, Spinner was in the exercise area with a few other rescued breeder dogs. A new family was interested in adopting Spinner, but Spinner showed little interest in them. Instead he walked over to Ann, looked at the large camera on her shoulder, and sat right down in front of her as if to say, "Take me home."

Two weeks later, Spinner came home to live with Ann, Penny, and Ann's other Golden Retriever, Breeze. Ann said that she was "only fostering" Spinner to get him housetrained, so that he would be more adoptable later. I must admit that I laughed when Ann told me this—I knew that Spinner had already found his new home!

Like a woman who claimed to forget the pain of childbirth and went on to have more children, Ann must have forgotten the struggles of her first weeks of life with Penny. Spinner presented his own stressful moments, too. Ann decided to use a crate to housetrain Spinner. She had an older style crate with a flimsy lock. The first night, Ann put Spinner into a crate in her master bedroom, a cozy place that gave Spinner just enough room to feel secure. When Ann closed the door to the crate, Spinner immediately tried to dig out of it. Demonstrating the same frantic determination that he used to try to open his kennel latch at DVGRR, Ann was afraid that Spinner might hurt himself. So she called me—at 11:00pm!

I sensed the same distress in Ann's voice that I heard when she first adopted Penny. I also knew that Ann did not sleep for the first three nights after she adopted Penny, and was concerned that Spinner might have the same effect. "Do you have a Kong®? Does he like peanut butter?" I asked. I had a feeling that Spinner would not give us any easy solutions to his anxiety.

Spinner not only needed a gradual introduction to his crate, he needed incentive to get in there. Together, Ann and I determined a strategy to get Spinner to go into his crate for small amounts of time by putting peanut butter into a Kong®, a hollow cone-shaped dog toy made for stuffing treats into it. When peanut butter is smeared inside, it takes most dogs a long time to lick it out. The peanut butter and Kong® worked together like a charm!

Although Ann did not sleep too well that first night, it demonstrated that they were certainly on the right track. Ann bought a new crate, and Spinner quickly became more comfortable in his new safe place in Ann's bedroom. A few days later, Ann shortened Spinner's name to Spin, from the '50s television show Spin and Marty (one more reason I believed that Spin was destined to live with Ann forever).

Spin's spinning ceased but he was still a very anxious fellow. He barked and paced if Ann left the house, even to step out onto the front porch to bring in her mail. Instead of crating him while she went out, Ann tried gating Spinner in the kitchen, thinking that it would give him a small space, which would facilitate housetraining, but also provide more room than a crate.

The gates were installed in Ann's kitchen when she adopted Penny. The large, decorative wrought iron gates were impenetrable. They worked great for Penny and Breeze. But Spin was a different dog. He barked and paced, possibly remembering his previous home and the ordeal in their kitchen. Ann put him in his crate again, where he seemed to feel more secure. With just a few more practices, Spin willingly went into his crate and quietly lay down. This is where he now stays when Ann leaves the house.

Spin's health was also an initial concern for Ann. He needed a rotten tooth pulled due to poor nutrition and lack of previous veterinary care. He also lacked stamina, possibly because he was never allowed out of his crate to run around. When Ann tried to take him for a walk, Spin labored along for about a block and then stopped and sat down. Ann was reluctant to force him to walk, so they would sit on someone else's lawn until he seemed ready to walk again. But Spin characteristically wagged his tail and looked happy to see anyone who drove or walked by.

Ann soon realized that Spin was still healing, so she didn't push him to take walks. Instead, Spin and the other dogs enjoyed playing in her large fenced backyard. Spin and Penny became the best of friends. They love to wrestle and romp in the yard. Breeze was also happy that Spin had arrived—Breeze was getting too old for such nonsense and didn't have to play with Penny anymore!

In the fall of 2007, Ann made it official and adopted Spin. He was finally in his forever home. Sadly, Breeze passed away shortly after Spin was adopted. But now, Spin's brow is no longer furrowed and worried, and his crooked face has noticeably straightened out. Spin will never look like a show dog, but his happiness remains infectious as he greets visitors with a jump that is still light as a feather, and a tail that wags his entire body. His fur is luxurious and his body is strong. He takes daily walks, with plenty of stamina to explore the neighborhood, where he greets people and other dogs with an obvious joy for life. He loves to visit with Ann's friend Maureen, who has a Golden named Seamus. Spin, Penny, and Seamus all play together in Maureen's yard.

And on their way back home, someone inevitably greets Ann and Spin and says, "What a beautiful dog!"

I'm Never Going Back in a Cage Again

Tips for Getting Your Dog to Walk Through Doorways

♥ Your dog needs to *want* to go through the doorway. Find something that most motivates your dog: Another dog, high value food, you!

♥ The best motivator is another dog (that's why it's best when breeder dogs live with another dog). Typically, the breeder dog will follow the other dog through the doorway.

♥ If you don't have another dog, or your dog still won't go through doorways, start slowly by luring your dog with a high value treat. Place the treat right at the doorway or hold the treat in your hand. Give the treat to your dog as he or she gradually gets closer to the doorway.

♥ Take it slow; work on it a little each day until your dog is successfully crossing thresholds.

Chapter Nine

I walk down one row of cages and see a litter of seven Jack Russell puppies nursing at their mother. She looks up at me but quickly turns her head away. She appears exhausted and defeated. She and her puppies occupy a pen that is larger than the cages and has a floor lined with straw...

HOLD IT!

Walking Through Doorways

The Introduction mentioned another odd but fairly consistent trait of breeder dogs: Fear of going through doorways. Dogs like Lady in chapter six typically stop before a threshold and will either not cross or hesitate to go through.

No one is really sure why. The simplest explanation may be the best: These dogs never had to pass through doorways in their breeding environment, so the confined feeling of the doorframe may make them uncomfortable. It is also possible that they may associate doorways with their crates opening and closing, and are afraid that the door may close on them. Sadly, we are not clued in about why these dogs react this way.

All we can do is work on remedying the problem. Some folks have sure found creative ways around it!

One Golden Retriever was surrendered to DVGRR during a monthly roundup and was adopted into her new home with a woman and her adult daughter. The dog found a comfortable place on a big khaki cotton dog bed nestled in front of a warm fireplace. She lay there for hours on her first day home—which sounds fine, except that she was frozen in fear.

Eventually, her adopters decided that she should go outside for a potty break. They placed her leash on her (thanks to help from DVGRR staff, she was one of the rare breeder dogs who walked nicely on a leash) and gently tried to lead her to their back yard.

She reached the double doors to the back yard and stopped. She "dug in her heels" and stubbornly, absolutely refused to move. Nothing—not chicken, cheese, dog treats, not tons of coaxing—persuaded this dog to move. How were they going to get her outside?

This is a prime example of how you must allow room for creativity when living with and training rescued breeder dogs. These clever adopters carried the dog's bed up to the doorway, and then placed the dog on top. Then they dragged the bed and the dog through the doorway. As soon as the bed cleared through the opening, the dog hopped off and ran around the yard!

Reentering the house was not as challenging because the dog wanted to get back to her safety zone; she hesitated but quickly scampered through the door, back into the house, and back onto her bed by the crackling, soothing fire.

Creativity

No matter how patient you are or how many of these suggestions you use, there may be times when none of them will work. In those times, you may need to get creative.

Many common tasks may require some ingenuity. These can include getting your dog to walk up and down steps, in and out of doors and through doorways, to walk on unfamiliar floor surfaces or to move on if your dog stops during a walk.

At first, you may have no other choice but to carry your dog through thresholds, across unfamiliar floor surfaces or up and down steps. If you do, use it as an opportunity to build your dog's confidence: Carry your dog only halfway then put down your dog and encouragingly lead him or her the rest of the way through. Even small successes can help build your dog's trust and confidence.

Puppy Mill Dogs SPEAK!

Chapter Ten

The area is covered with feces. Pieces of feces and cheap food float in the metal pan of water in the corner. A similar small pen holds a litter of Golden Retriever puppies who happily come over to greet me. Their tails have no fur on them, and patches of fur are missing from other areas of their bodies. In the corner of their pen lies their dead mother. Flies swirl and buzz around her body...

DON'T MAKE ANY CHANGES

Consistency and Routine

The other vital characteristic of rescued breeder dogs like Buster (chapter five) is that they desperately cling to consistency and routine. If something changes in their environment or schedule, they are likely to shut down. If your dog encounters something during his or her walk that has not been there before, for example, your dog may either shut down or try to retreat back to his or her safety zone. One breeder dog adopter tells the story of how her dog flattened out on the ground when she saw balloons floating in the air, decorating a nearby mailbox.

Your world is a new, strange place to rescued breeder dogs. Changes within your home, such as adding or rearranging furniture, new window treatments, and other modifications, can also evoke fear reactions. One adopted, rescued breeder dog suddenly refused to go outside and began having potty accidents in the house after she had lived in that home for many months and had been perfectly housetrained up until that point.

Her adopters called me in for a consultation. After much examination—and literally crawling on the floor to follow the path that their dog would take to go outside—I asked her adopters if anything had recently changed in their dog's path. I noticed the tablecloth hanging from the dining room table and asked, "Has that always been there?"

A knowing smile came upon the wife's face when she realized that these accidents started to happen right when she switched from placemats on the table to the tablecloth. Their dog saw this strange new thing hanging in her path and it freaked her out. The tablecloth was removed and the accidents stopped. This family now says that it is a small sacrifice to do without a tablecloth!

It can prove quite problematic if your dog is accustomed to having someone with him or her most of the time, and then is frequently left alone. Schedule alterations can throw your dog for a loop as well. If your dog is accustomed to getting up or having a walk at a certain time, and then these times change, your dog may exhibit signs of stress and even regress in their progress. Extreme changes of this type would be very stressful for any dog, but especially so for a breeder dog.

Buster, for example, has a hard time adjusting when the clocks are set ahead one hour each spring. Before the time change, it would still be light outside when Chris got home from work. Chris would walk Buster and then feed him. When it was time for Buster's after-dinner bathroom walk, it would be dark outside.

Don't Make Any Changes

But after the time change, it was already dark when Chris got home from work. When Chris approached Buster with the leash, Buster grew confused and seemed to anxiously fret, "It must be time for my after-dinner walk because there's Daddy with the leash and it's dark outside. But how can it be time for my walk in the dark outside if I haven't eaten dinner yet?" Getting Buster to walk outside just takes a little more patience and creativity than usual for a few weeks after these time changes.

Holidays are not only "the most wonderful time of the year"—they're also a time of year that often adversely affects dogs' routines and environments. You and your family may be busy with shopping, party-going, decorating, and other activities, which can leave your dog alone longer than usual or reduce their amount of exercise. Adding decorations such as a Christmas tree to your home may also distress your dog. Some breeder dogs will regress during these holidays. Housetraining accidents may occur. Your dog may refuse to come into rooms decorated for the holidays.

But the presence of holiday visitors in your home is even more problematic for rescued breeder dogs. This increased activity may overwhelm your dog; if your dog is still wary of strangers, this may raise the likelihood of your dog trying to flee from your home, or shutting down in fear.

So please: Give your dog special care and consideration during the holidays to minimize their holiday stress.

Structure, Routine, Consistency

Interestingly, many breeder dogs who exhibit signs of extreme trauma may act somewhat like people suffering from obsessive-compulsive disorder (OCD), Down's syndrome or autism.

Some OCD sufferers must know that things are always in their proper place. For instance, some will insist that the chairs around the dining room table must go back precisely into their indentations in the carpet after they've been moved. These OCD sufferers literally cannot function until such a "wrong" is righted.

People suffering from Down's syndrome or autism typically need to know that they will awaken at the same time every day, for example, or that Tuesday is shopping day, or that we always have pizza on Saturday. Deviation from this routine can greatly distress these people.

Breeder dogs exhibit this same sort of behavior by freezing in place if surrounded by new or unfamiliar circumstances. For example, one breeder dog took six months before she could be walked outside her yard on a leash. Her first few tentative times, she needed another dog with her. She seemed to settle into a route, a quick loop around the block. After several weeks of success, her adopter decided to switch routes. When they took that first different turn, the dog froze in her tracks. No amount of verbal encouragement, cheese or even chicken could lure that dog to move. Her adopter finally nudged the dog back into their original route, then they quickly continued home.

Similarly, a consistent schedule will help your adopted breeder dog adjust to life in your home: Get up at the same time, feed meals at the same time, walk at the same time, every day. This not only gives your dog a sense of security, it helps with housetraining!

As with any dog, consistent language is also important. Pick one name for your dog and stick to it. Avoid generic nicknames like "honey" or "sweetie." Calling your dog by only one name will help your dog recognize when you are calling. Teach your

Structure, Routine, Consistency
(Continued)

dog the proper words for common objects and tasks, such as outside, potty, and dinner, and the usual obedience words such as sit, down, come, and stay. Consistency is important. Inconsistency will bring confusion, and confusion will evoke fear.

Make sure that family members, neighbors, friends and anyone else who interact with your dog consistently use these same words. It will be comforting for your dog to be able to recognize what they are saying and doing if they use the same consistent language. If you use the word "outside" to cue your dog to go outside for potty, for example, and someone else says "door," your dog will not understand that "door" means "outside." Even worse, the other person may become frustrated with your dog, which your dog will sense and become even more confused and frightened.

Preventing Escapes

As we've learned throughout this book, a common trait of rescued breeder dogs is fear. The least little noise, unfamiliar situation, approach of a stranger or just the presentation of an opportunity may cause the dog to try to flee. Some easy steps are important to assure that your dog stays safely with you.

- ♥ When walking outside of any fenced area, attach two leashes to your dog, one to the dog's body harness and another to the dog's collar. Hold one leash in each hand.

- ♥ In your home, ensure that your dog is gated or behind a securely closed door when any outside door is opened to a non-fenced in area.

- ♥ When transporting your dog in the car, ensure that all windows are closed enough that your dog cannot squeeze through. Do not open the doors until your dog is secure and the leashes are in your hands.

- ♥ If you have a garage, if possible always put your dog into the car in the garage with the garage door closed.

- ♥ When entering your house after your dog is out for a leashed walk, keep your dog on the leash until all doors to the outside are securely closed.

Chapter Eleven

I've seen more than enough and turn, aghast and afraid of being caught, to run away. But love for animals stops me in my tracks.

GET ME OUTTA HERE!

Flight Risk

Because of the terror that some rescued puppy mill dogs can associate with their new environments—the people, the house, the strange noises, etc.—they have been known to run away if not securely kept on a leash or within a fence. Like Buddy in chapter one, these dogs have a tendency to flee if something frightens them. Some of these dogs will run away from the house, the place they are afraid of; other dogs will run toward the house, the place where they know that they are safe.

Due to this unpredictability, I strongly recommend that adopted puppy mill dogs live in a home with a fenced-in yard. If this is not possible, then extreme diligence with keeping your dog securely on a leash becomes even more important.

But even a fence is not enough to keep some dogs in. In 2006, one breeder dog was adopted from DVGRR into what seemed to be the perfect scenario, a home with a fenced-in yard and another dog. But this breeder dog was one of the most fearful I have ever met. She would not come to anyone. She spent her days plastered into the corner of the yard, as far away from people as possible. In her new home, she attached herself to the wife of the family but remained terrified of her husband. If she could not be in the yard, she hid under the wife's desk.

One day, she found a hole under the split rail/chicken wire fence and dug her way out. Her adopters did not know she was gone until it was too late and she was nowhere to be found. They placed frantic phone calls to DVGRR and everyone they knew to help look for her.

She remained missing for almost a week until a volunteer from DVGRR took his dog for just one more search, and found her. This volunteer led his dog back to her home, and she followed. Her family had already reinforced every area of the fence in the hope that she would return and never escape again.

Something similar happened in November 2008 when Oscar, a DVGRR Golden Retriever being fostered by Maureen McCulloch, escaped from a car.

Oscar's Great Escape

The picture of a stunningly beautiful Golden Retriever on the DVGRR website told only half of Oscar's story. He looked perfect on the outside. But under his luxurious, creamy blonde coat, and behind those soft brown eyes, was a dog who was afraid of the world.

Puppy mill breeder dog behavior ranges from most fearful and scared to friendly and uninhibited, depending upon their genetic disposition and how they were treated at the puppy mill. Judging from Oscar's demeanor, his seven years in the puppy mill must have been pure hell.

Despite several months of rehabilitation efforts by DVGRR staff, Oscar remained timid and extremely cautious of people. Donna Baker, DVGRR's Adoption Manager, realized that Oscar had progressed as far as he could at their kennel facility. Oscar needed to live in a home, with people, exposed to life.

Maureen McCulloch spotted Oscar's beautiful picture on the DVGRR website. But it was the description accompanying his photo that caught her attention. Maureen works with autistic and special needs children. She knew that she could use this expertise to help Oscar by fostering him, and applied to serve as his foster caregiver. Soon thereafter, she received a call from DVGRR to do just that. "I think we were definitely meant to be together," Maureen says.

Oscar came home to live with Maureen, her husband, and two children, in mid-June 2008. The very first day together offered a preview of their new life with Oscar.

Oscar orchestrated a breakout from the back of her Volvo station wagon. Because he will not walk on a leash, Oscar needed to be carried from the DVGRR kennel, across the parking lot to Maureen's car—losing his bowels the entire way. He was gently placed in the back seat and then he panicked. Oscar squeezed out the window (which was only open about a third of the way), and took off running. Luckily, he stayed close on the DVGRR property because he knew it as his "safe place."

Since Oscar feels more comfortable around other dogs, the staff brought a few other dogs outside; Oscar followed them back to the kennel, where he was recaptured. With Oscar safely back in her Volvo, Maureen bravely moved forward with her decision to foster him. Off they went to her Freehold, New Jersey, home. But the whole time she was thinking, "What am I doing?"

At Maureen's home, Oscar practically lived in his crate for the first month, and then found a "safe place" in the hallway near the front door, and another in the bathroom right next to the back door. Despite the efforts of Maureen and her entire family, Oscar never attempted to explore their house. His only goal seemed to be to get out of there. Every opening of the back door, no matter how slight, created an opportunity for Oscar to bolt out into the fenced-in back yard. Once Oscar was outside, it took hours to coax him back into the house. One day, it took Maureen six hours to get Oscar back inside her home! After that, Maureen began keeping Oscar on a long nylon leash so that she could get him back inside more quickly.

The family was unable to touch Oscar for weeks. He fled or shut down in fear. In July, Maureen decided that Oscar needed relief from such extreme anxiety, and got him a prescription for an anti-anxiety medication. This helped Oscar to relax and accept gradual touching, but only from Maureen. Maureen used very short periods of touching, and worked up to fifteen minutes of massage each day. Oscar even progressed to seeking out affection from Maureen, but only just for a second, and only when Maureen was alone. Oscar remained quite terrified of men.

Oscar's refusal to walk on a leash presented a problem, such as when he needed to go to the veterinarian's office. His first visit was uneventful; Maureen's husband and son carried Oscar to and from the car (again losing his bowels the whole way). But Oscar got sick a few months later. He was vomiting and not eating. Maureen scheduled a vet appointment for the end of her work day, and arranged for her husband and son to bring Oscar from their home to meet her there.

Her husband, son, and Oscar arrived first. Oscar's fear and adrenaline had combined to break the ring on his collar that was attached to the leash. No one but Oscar knew that it was broken (and Oscar wasn't telling). Before Maureen showed up, her husband and son opened the back door to their car to walk Oscar into the veterinarian's office. When the car door opened, Oscar slipped his broken collar ring and took off running. Maureen's husband and son tried to chase him, but because Oscar was so terrified of men, the more they chased him, the further he ran out of sight.

Thus began six very long days of all-out searching, desperately trying to find a fugitive who fled whenever a person approached. Maureen called in every possible resource, including local animal shelters, police departments, DVGRR staff, and local veterinarians. She posted flyers, knocked on doors, and placed ads on Craigslist and other lost pet websites. She even contacted animal search and rescue specialists who brought in trained tracking dogs, but Oscar's scent was too faint to follow due to the amount of time that had passed.

Maureen and her team searched for days. There were several confirmed sightings, and a few wild goose chases. Throughout her ordeal, Maureen was accompanied by Lynda Neff of Golden Re-Triever Rescue Inc.—New Jersey and Lynda's Golden Retriever, D. Jay. Lynda walked through the woods in the area where Oscar escaped. As a rule, puppy mill dogs will follow other dogs when they are frightened, so Lynda brought along her dogs on the search in the hopes that Oscar would see the other dogs and emerge from hiding.

On the sixth day, when Maureen was just about running out of hope, Maureen received a telephone call from the police. A dog had been found hiding in the back yard of a woman who, coincidentally, is also involved in animal rescue. It was six miles away from the area he had disappeared. Indeed, it was Oscar!

It remains a mystery, however, how Oscar got into that yard—it was fenced in, and no holes were found that Oscar might have dug to get into the yard. It is possible that someone found Oscar and placed him in this woman's yard because they knew she was involved with animal rescue. Which leads to another mystery: How did they manage to catch him?

Safely back home, Oscar was exhausted, hungry, covered with ticks and, thankfully, unharmed.

Six days out on his own seemed to make Oscar appreciate his new home and family. He was a changed boy. Maureen suggests that Oscar realized this: "The real world can be pretty scary." Oscar now bounds back into the house from Maureen's back yard, ventures into the kitchen (where he had never gone before), joins the family at dinnertime, and even lies on the rug in their TV room.

Even so, Oscar remains ever watchful and on alert and will dart away if frightened. But Maureen has seen so much progress, and in that progress finds more hope.

"The whole ordeal with Oscar has changed me forever. I have much more faith in life and that all the things that happen to us are for a reason," Maureen says. "And the abundance of support from so many people is beyond anyone's imagination. Oscar has changed me—and of course aged me a little, too!" Oscar was found the day before Thanksgiving. So there was much for Maureen to be thankful for that Thanksgiving, of course.

"Working with Oscar and watching him take his slow little steps toward becoming a normal dog is one of the most rewarding experiences in my life!" marvels Maureen. She is most grateful for this outpouring of help and support and is eternally indebted to Lynda Neff for being there for her. Maureen also sends special "thank you's" to Debra Kourtz, Colleen Bezanson and her Irish Setter, Maggie, and Lynn Conover and her Golden Retriever, Kolby also a DVGRR dog, for the endless amount of hours they combed the woods and neighborhoods in search of that tall handsome blond, Oscar; and to Donna Baker, for all her supportive phone calls to Maureen, encouraging her to find the strength to forge on and not give up. So many people learned a very important life lesson through their search for Oscar: Never, never, give up. Keep the faith!

We can learn many things from Oscar's escape. And we can be relieved that Oscar's story has a happy ending!

Chapter Twelve

I know that I need to do something to help these defenseless dogs who humans have domesticated and taught to love and trust us.

IT'S TIME FOR PROGRESS

Leadership and Training Principles for All Dogs

Even though their previous bad experiences have taught breeder dogs that humans are to be feared, they may still be able to consider humans part of their hierarchical social structure—often referred to as their pack—with lots of help from us. Once your dog has begun to live in your home and to trust you, his or her reliance on social structure will become even more evident.

There also comes a time when your rescued breeder dog must stop being coddled, when you need to apply leadership principles or obedience training. These dogs need us to be their leaders and give their lives structure, so that they do not become even more anxious than they already are and can start being "normal dogs." They need to know where they fit into their new social structure, which is a natural instinct for dogs.

There has been much debate among animal behavior researchers about the origins of dogs, whether they truly are pack animals, and what kind of social structure they require. Some say that dogs evolved from wolves, the epitome of pack animals; others say there is no evidence for this evolution, and that dogs are a separate species. Studies indicate that dogs do not form the same pack bonds for hunting and raising young that wolves do. If this is true, to treat dogs as pack animals is a mistake.

However, the evidence does show that dogs respond to traditional pack hierarchy, in which one dog has the leadership position that is respected by the others. Consequently, treating dogs as if they are pack animals has its merits, even though "dog packs" and "wolf packs" remain very different things.

For example, wolves hunt together in order to bring down the very large animals—such as deer, elk, and other large mammals—they need to survive. If they did not have cooperative hunting skills, it would not be possible for wolves to kill such large animals. In the hunt, each member of the wolf pack has his or her own job: One chases the prey, others circle around to block its escape, while others begin to grab at the prey's legs to force it down. The most dominant member of the pack eats first and chases away the most timid in the group, regardless of how helpful that member was in bringing down their prey.

The more dominant wolf shows that he's in charge in other ways: He chases other males away from the female he wishes to mate with and will either pin down his opponent, or simply stand over him, during play. The more dominant wolf generally does not allow his opponent to flip him onto his back. He infrequently needs to resort to physical violence to demonstrate his status.

Regardless of their origin, there is no doubt that the earliest dogs bonded to humans by scavenging the garbage left behind by humans. Dogs quickly found that if they hung around the humans, they would get a free meal! The dogs' social structure emerged as the dogs frequented the garbage dump: The most dominant dog was able to fend off others to get to the food first; the more timid dogs were not as successful in gaining access to premium scraps. Eating the leftovers did not give these more timid dogs enough nutrition to make them strong enough to physically challenge the leader.

A social hierarchy formed among the dogs at the dump as a result. This structure is distinctly different from a pack structure. Pack structure implies cooperative skills (such as those used for hunting); a hierarchical structure is more competitive and much less cooperative.

Nonetheless, dogs definitely have instincts to be part of a pack. In human terms, we call a pack our family. Dogs are social animals just like people, which is why they have historically bonded to us so well.

All Are Not Created Equal

First, let's explore how the dogs' social hierarchy works and how humans fit into it. The first and most important thing to learn is that dogs do not think in terms of everyone being equal, as most humans do. We are mostly taught that we should all get along with each other, and that no person is better or worse than another. But dogs don't think that way. Dogs think in terms of a hierarchy, where there is a leader and the rest of the pack falls into a fluid order under the leader, all the way down to the most subservient dog. The leader is called the "alpha" and the lowest ranking member of the pack is the "omega." Every dog in between can have varying degrees of authority, and might even occasionally challenge the alpha for leadership.

Most breeder dogs exhibit the characteristics of an omega dog for at least some time after their rescue from the puppy mill. They are very timid and will quickly give in to any challenge by either freezing in place or dropping to the ground, and often urinate as a sign that they are not a threat.

Dogs recognize and respect the alpha personality of the group and allow the alpha to have the first turn at all resources. What is a resource? It's anything that is desired by the dog. Food is the most obvious resource. Access to toys, walks, and the yard, the ability to sleep on furniture and the bed, and attention from humans, are also resources to your dog. In a true pack, the most dominant member will have first access to all of these resources. Then others will follow.

Your dog should never play the lead role in your home situation. Unfortunately, today's society seems to allow our dogs the same privileges as our children. Many dogs are treated more like children and given free access to all resources—food/treats, human affection, and more toys than you can imagine. If you or another human does not control access to these resources, your dog will take over as leader. After all, the one who controls the resources is the one in charge!

It's Time For Progress

Giving your rescued breeder dog free access to all resources places him or her in the position of leader. Being a leader is not in your breeder dog's best interest. Your dog is already stressed. Add on the stress of managing the resources—otherwise known as being in charge—and you'll have a really stressed and anxious dog.

Instead, your dog needs you to be the provider of resources—the leader. You can begin to be the leader as soon as your dog begins to settle into your home. Here are methods that all dogs will recognize to show that you're in charge:

1. At mealtime, ask your dog to wait for about 15—30 seconds while you hold the dog's dish, and then place the dish on the floor.
2. Ensure that your dog does not run in and out of doors, or up and down steps, in front of you. Of course, you are probably laughing that your dog will not use the steps or freezes before going out of doorways! But one of these days, your dog will do these things effortlessly. That's the time to teach your dog to wait for you.
3. Restrain yourself from giving your dog too much affection, especially when your dog asks for it. It's simple human nature to feel very sorry for the unspeakable trauma that your dog endured at the puppy mill, but no amount of love and affection can take that away. Providing leadership and structure will make it better. Deliver attention and affection to your dog when you want to initiate it, not when your dog demands it.

4. Discourage your dog from taking residence on your bed or furniture. As tempting as it may be to allow your dog to lie with you, this is generally not a good idea. When dogs are on the furniture, they control these resources. If you really, really want your dog on the furniture with you, be the initiator by inviting your dog to come up with you instead of allowing your dog to just jump up on his or her own.
5. During walks, ensure that your dog is not way out in front of you, thus leading the walk. Keep your dog close to you so that he or she can hear and follow your direction. Sit and wait at intersections until you say it's okay to move on.

Physical Posture and Body Language

In the dog world, physical postures have so much more meaning than they do to humans, because dogs cannot talk like we can. The quicker you learn dog language, the better you will be at communicating with your dog.

Humans can inadvertently give dogs threatening signals that we are in charge. For example, dogs consider direct and persistent eye contact to be a threat. Never stare directly at a breeder dog if you want to gain his or her trust. Instead, glance sideways and down when looking at him or her. Another direct threat to a dog can be your simple physical approach. Walking head-on up to a dog is very threatening to them. In order not to scare your dog, approach from the side and make a wide semi-circle while approaching.

It's Time For Progress

Some old fashioned dog trainers and even one popular television personality employ physical tactics to show that they're in charge. Avoid these fear-evoking methods by all means—not only for puppy mill dogs but for all dogs. One such tactic is the "alpha roll," whereby the human rolls the dog onto his or her back or side, holds them there and forces the dog to lie still. Unfortunately, many years ago researchers were studying wolves and mistakenly determined that this alpha roll was how one wolf established himself the leader. This misconception has since been recanted by the group who documented this observation.

More recent studies have shown that a true leader who is respected by the pack does not need to resort to alpha rolls. The pack already knows by other more benevolent actions that he is the leader. Sadly, some dog trainers and so-called dog experts are still uninformed and teach the alpha roll to show leadership to dogs. Using an alpha roll on a puppy mill dog—or on any shy, fearful dog, for that matter—will have detrimental effects. This dog will become even more fearful and mistrusting of humans.

Other fear-based methods of dog training involve grabbing the dog by parts of the dog's body. Scruffing is a method of grabbing the dog by the back of his or her neck (scruff) to correct the dog if he or she is misbehaving. It is intended to mimic the mother dog's way of correcting her pups by picking one up with her teeth by the back of the neck and removing the pup from the others if that pup is being bad. It is meant to be a timeout, not a punishment. Another force-based method to correct a dog is by grabbing the dog by the jowls (the dog's cheeks) and telling the dog, "No!"

There are several problems with these methods: First, dogs don't have hands. Scruffing them or grabbing them by the jowls may only teach them to fear our hands. Already fearful dogs will become more fearful from these aggressive approaches and will not trust you. Breeder dogs are familiar with being "man-handled" by peoples' hands. It's a large part of what made them so fearful in the first place. More fear-based handling will not help.

Training

You may be thinking that some of this sounds very nice, but my dog does not even know basic commands such as sit and stay. It is time—your dog needs obedience training! However, I do not like to use the words "obedience training." I prefer to call it "communication skills" because dog training is really teaching your dog how to understand your communication with them. We need to help your dog understand that *this word is* associated with *this activity*—that *sit* means to *put your backside down on the ground*. Otherwise, your dog will only hear "Blah blah blah" and will have no idea what you want him or her to do.

It is extremely unfair to not train a dog in our language. Without that training, your dog is like a stranger wandering through a foreign land without knowing the native tongue.

It's Time For Progress

You generally have two options when choosing how to have your dog trained, private lessons or group classes. There are pros and cons to both. Your choice is very important for your shy, rescued breeder dog.

The very best reason for attending a group class is the socialization aspect. Your dog will get to meet other dogs and maybe even get a chance to play with them. Your dog will also be exposed to lots of other people. This can be good or bad, depending upon how well your dog does around strangers.

I have only known a few breeder dogs, through my own experience, who did really well in a group obedience class. It took a few sessions for one male to relax. If anyone approached him during his first two sessions, he would flatten himself out on the floor like a pancake and squeeze his eyes shut. Being approached by people was just too much for him. But at his third session, the instructor suggested that everyone take turns coming over to this dog and slowly giving him a very high quality treat. Surprisingly, it worked! As you can imagine, this dog was not too highly traumatized so his recovery was not so lengthy. I would not recommend trying this with a very shy and fearful dog.

If you can afford to hire a qualified trainer or behavior specialist to visit your home to work with your dog, this is probably your best option. This gives your dog the opportunity to focus on learning instead of watching out for approaching strangers. But carefully do your homework to choose the right trainer. Not every trainer knows how to deal with a breeder dog, and many have no idea how to work with their particular issues.

Getting referrals from the place where you adopted your rescued dog, your veterinarian, and knowledgeable friends, is a great place to start. Call each referral and ask about their experience in working with unsocialized or abused dogs. Please select a trainer who uses positive, rewards-based training methods. Steer clear of trainers who advocate using choke or prong collars, or any form of physical punishment. Please.

Then take the training process very slowly. Instead of trying to work on several commands in one session, work on just one or two. Remember that your dog is trying to not only learn your verbal language but your physical language, too. Your dog may still think that hands are only used for hitting and grabbing. Take this opportunity to help your dog associate your hands with good things.

Training is also a great opportunity to incorporate overcoming fears. For instance, one rescued Golden Retriever breeder dog named Molly was making wonderful progress after just one week of living in her new home. For the first few days, Molly would not venture out of the family room onto the hardware floor in the nearby kitchen. After a week, she was getting braver and started to walk on the hardware floor but would not come all the way into the kitchen. This kitchen, although large, was divided by an island. It's possible that it might have felt too confining, or just too overwhelming, for her.

We decided to try to teach Molly how to lie down. Using a very high quality food (canned chicken), I coaxed Molly to come into the kitchen area, to determine her boundaries. Then I asked Molly to sit, which she had already learned and loved to obey. With just three tries, this smart and sweet girl learned how to lie down.

With every try, I gradually scooted myself further back into the kitchen area. Before she realized it, Molly was in the area that just a few minutes earlier had frightened her! You could almost see the pride shine in her eyes when Molly was able to accomplish this seemingly small yet significant feat.

Creative Games

Everyone learns best when they are having fun and are not under stress, so make your dog's training fun! There are several ways that games can help your dog to learn, gain confidence, and help forge a bond between you as well.

One of my favorite games is hide and seek. Begin in a room in your house where your dog is comfortable. Then hide behind a chair, sofa, or in a closet. Call your dog to you, and watch him or her try to find you. When you're found, act very happy, and praise your dog. Most dogs react with excitement to this game.

Now move your game to a fenced-in area outside. Find a tree or a small structure like a shed and hide behind it. Call your dog to you, and happily praise him or her when they find you!

Another fun indoor game is something that I call "find it." Place treats in various locations all around a room—under toys, in a Kong® toy, on the steps, scattered about the floor. Then tell your dog, in an excited voice, to "Find it!" As your dog finds each treat, act very happy, and praise your dog.

Since many rescued breeder dogs are uncomfortable with human contact and may freeze if someone leans over to praise or pet them, teaching your dog to go between your legs can be another helpful exercise. It aids in building trust. It may take many patient tries, but gradually your dog will learn to confidently go through your legs.

Stand with your legs rather wide apart, and lure your dog close to your legs using a high quality treat. Simply pet your dog while they stand close to you. Gradually, keep moving closer, and guide your legs around your dog. Give treats when your dog stands between your legs. Use your best judgment on how comfortable your dog is in this position.

Then begin to lure your dog to go all the way through by holding the treats behind you, so that your dog has to go through your legs to reach their treat. Even if your dog just stands there, continue to praise and give him or her treats. Remember, even very small steps are very significant. Patiently continue to lure your dog to pass through your legs until your dog willingly scoots through them.

If your dog is not willing to go through your legs, you can try to very slowly lift your leg over your dog's head to simulate the dog passing through your legs. Act happy and continue to lavish praise. If this exercise seems to cause your dog more stress, discontinue it.

Even though this is not really a game, you can even make it fun when your dog simply looks at you. Breeder dogs can be extremely shy creatures who are unwilling to look you or anyone in the eye. So any time you can catch your dog looking anywhere near your face, give him or her a bright happy smile and a, "Good dog!" This will encourage your dog to look at your more often, and to feel more comfortable making eye contact with people.

Creative Games—Shaping

There is a method of training dogs called shaping for when you believe your dog is ready to learn more. Shaping teaches your dog how to behave a certain way by incrementally rewarding small actions that lead up to the desired behavior until your dog can perform that behavior.

Let's say that you want to teach your dog how to lie down but your dog is resistant. First, ask your dog to sit. Place a high quality treat in front of your dog's nose. Let your dog smell it and show interest in taking it. Slowly move the treat down to the floor in front of your dog. Move it between his or her legs, or out in front of their legs, so that your dog must stretch down to get their treat. Some dogs will drop to the floor; others will resist and pop back up. For these resistant dogs, shaping helps.

When you place the treat between your dog's legs or out in front of them, praise and treat your dog for even the slightest movement down toward the floor. For each try, and for every time your dog gets closer to the floor, praise and treat. Most dogs will begin to retain the idea that you want them to be lying down. This is shaping.

Creative Games—Targeting

Another very fun activity is called targeting. By teaching your dog to touch the end of a stick (you can use a yardstick, a ruler, or any similar object), you can point that stick toward anything and teach your dog numerous tricks.

Targeting is used to teach dogs who assist the handicapped how to turn on light switches and close doors. Once your dog can touch a target, you can teach him or her many different behaviors. It is limited only by your imagination!

Here's how you can teach your dog through targeting: Place whatever target object you choose to use (i.e., your yardstick, ruler, other stick, etc.) within a few inches of your dog's nose. Wait for your dog to move his or her nose near the target, then praise and treat your dog. Gradually, your dog will begin to understand that he or she gets rewarded for touching the target, and will consistently touch it. Continue to praise and treat as this happens.

Then pick the behavior that you want your dog to learn, such as ringing a doorbell near a doorknob. Place the target on the bell. Continue to praise and treat when your dog noses the target.

Next, add a command (such as "Ring the bell!") when your dog consistently touches his or her nose to the target near the bell.

Then, remove the target but continue to issue the command, "Ring the bell!" Your dog should continue to touch his or her nose to the bell. Well done! Continue to praise and treat!

Creative Games—Agility

The sport of agility is very popular with dog lovers. Agility is essentially a game where your dog runs an obstacle course. The course consists of going through jumps and tunnels, walking up and down an A-frame, walking up and down a teeter-totter, weaving through poles, and jumping through tires. The course is laid out in a pattern and the dog must follow their owner's directions in order to complete the course in its proper sequence.

The challenge this presents for dogs is two-fold: Learning how to master the equipment first, then listening to their owner for the proper order in which to run the course. For a scared dog who lacks confidence, an agility course can be a very frightening thing. But in very small doses it can be a confidence builder.

Many countries, and most areas of the United States, offer agility classes either at dog training schools or at clubs that specialize in agility. Teaching agility is a specialty with which not all dog trainers have experience. Refer to the Resources section in the back of this book for assistance in finding a qualified school or club.

Another option is to purchase a home agility kit, which you can usually find in pet catalogs or on the internet. Home agility kits usually include jumps, weave poles, and tunnels, plus instructions on how to train your dog on the equipment.

Either option, if taken slowly, will help your dog to learn and become more confident. It will also increase the bond between you!

Creative Games—Clicker Training

Clicker training is another method of training dogs that has become increasingly popular. The scientific term for it is "operant conditioning," and it has been used for many years to train dolphins and whales.

You can purchase a clicker at any pet supply or even a party supply store. The "clicker" is a small plastic box with a metal strip that makes a sharp, distinct clicking sound when it is pushed then released. Its value is that this unique sound does not get lost in the babble of words that we constantly throw at our dogs. It reacts faster than you can say "Good dog!" and allows you to mark with great precision the exact behavior you are trying to reinforce with your dog. When used in tandem with something that your dog already finds reinforcing (like food), the clicker becomes a powerful tool for shaping behavior.

The sound of a clicker is very distinctive, and grabs the dog's attention. As you pair the sound of the clicker with a reward, your dog will begin to associate its sound with something pleasant. Eventually, you may even be able to eliminate the treats and use only the clicker as the reward, which comes in handy if you have a lot of training to do and don't wish to fatten up your dog with too many treats.

Begin your clicker training with easy to learn activities and then build upon them. You will first need to establish the association of something pleasant with the sound of the clicker. What motivates your dog the best? Is it food, or praise, or affection, or something else? Then start to practice the clicking and rewarding combination. Simply get your dog's attention, click, and reward. Remember: Be absolutely certain that you give your dog the reward immediately after you click so that your dog learns to associate hearing the click with receiving the reward. Practice this until your dog knows that every click comes with a reward thereafter.

Then, try "sit" as a start. Keep a watchful eye on your dog and if you happen to catch him or her starting to sit, immediately click and then reward. You must click the very instant that your dog performs the desired behavior (in this case, when your dog sits down). If you do not, your dog will become confused and think that you are rewarding him or her for a different behavior. Continue to practice this until your dog sits consistently. Attach the "sit" command at the instance your dog's backside hits the floor so that the dog associates the word with the action.

Learning is also enhanced when you present rewards at intervals. This way, your dog cannot predict when their reward is coming and will be all the more excited to perform the behavior. For example, as your dog is learning to sit, begin to click and treat every other time that your dog sits, and not every time. Then advance to every third time, every fourth time, or even vary it—every third time, then the second time, then the fourth time, and so on.

Be aware that some breeder dogs may be frightened by the sound of the clicker. If so, it's best to discontinue this activity.

Other Fun Activities

You have a growing number of options for places to play and bond with your dog. Dog parks seem to be springing up all over the place. A dog park is a designated fenced-in area where dogs can play and run off-leash, so long as their owners remain close by and are attentive. Interacting with other dogs is always a welcome event for rescued breeder dogs, and it gives them a chance to be around new people as well.

A dog park may be overwhelming for some dogs, so please approach this carefully. Also remember that dog parks are not monitored. Therefore, you may encounter other dogs whose behaviors may not be appropriate. Remain aware of how other dogs behave toward your dog and break up any overly rough play or aggressive incidents. Your little angel of a dog may be a perpetrator, too, so monitor your own dog's behavior just as closely.

If it is possible, frequently invite people to visit your home. This will help your dog grow more comfortable around strangers and accustomed to greeting new faces. When your visitors arrive, make sure that your dog is in a quiet and comfortable place, away from the door. Wait until your visitors have settled in, and then let your dog out to meet them. Give your guests high quality treats with which to greet your dog. If they are willing, you can even ask your guests to command your dog to sit or stay. All these things will help your dog to relax and trust the new faces in your home.

Rehabilitative and Reading Therapists

If you have the time, disposition, and inclination, many rescued breeder dogs—because of their sweet nature—also make wonderful therapy dogs. A therapy dog visits hospitals, nursing homes, and similar places, any place where the presence of a pet can help people to feel better. Many sick children can be cheered by the visit of a pet, or a regularly scheduled visit can give the elderly something to look forward to each week. Some of these places will require that you get your dog a special certification to serve as this type of therapy dog; others may not be as stringent. If you are interested in helping your dog grow through performing this type of service, check with the facility you wish to visit. Most will be very happy to explain their requirements.

The experience of completing therapy dog training will help your dog become socialized and overcome his or her fears. The soft look on the face of most puppy mill dogs, and the compassion it evokes, is so helpful to people who are facing their own struggles. How can I describe a rescued puppy mill dog's energy? It's...calm, for the most part, once they've overcome their fears, and introducing that kind of energy into a place like a retirement home, rehabilitation center, or hospital, has a calming effect on people. Many rescued breeder dogs would make tremendous therapy dogs IF they've reached that point in their own healing process.

These dogs are only there to give the patients love. There's just something almost spiritual about petting a dog. They're so unconditional and non-judgmental. They're what we should all be to each other, really, except that we can't put our egos aside like dogs can. They can bring peace to us.

Dogs also participate in programs that assist children with their reading skills. The child is paired up with and reads to a dog, which feels much less threatening to the child than reading to an adult or other person. The child knows that the dog is not judgmental and therefore reads more comfortably. A rescued breeder dog would love this type of quiet activity, and it exposes them to new people and places.

You can not only make a difference in the life of your adopted, rescued breeder dog—you can help your dog make a difference in someone else's life, too.

Please refer to the **Resources** section for more information on therapy dog and reading programs.

Chapter Thirteen

HEALTH ISSUES OF PUPPY MILL BREEDER DOGS

Due to the lack of healthcare and poor nutrition while kept captive in puppy mills, many breeder dogs present health challenges to rescue organizations, shelters, and their eventual adopters. The previous chapters mostly discussed everything you need to know about the behavioral issues of rescued puppy mill breeder dogs and how to help them. But the health problems that many bring with them from the puppy mill can be as problematic as these quirky behaviors. Knowing the background of these issues will help potential adopters know what to expect and assist with communicating these issues to your dog's veterinarian to optimize their treatment.

Of course, there are varying degrees of severity of puppy mill conditions around the country. But one thing is common and predictable: The food is very poor quality. Puppy mill owners want to invest as little money as possible—minimizing their investment means maximizing their profit. Many puppy mills feed their dogs the same feed as their livestock, which is usually grains, or scraps of other food. Clearly, these dogs do not receive enough of the high-quality protein required to keep carnivores healthy. This poor nutrition ultimately manifests itself through various health issues, including sparse coat, skin irritations, rotten teeth, lowered immune system, vision problems, and more.

Teeth

Are you familiar with the water bottles used in hamster or rabbit cages? Many puppy mills use these same bottles to give water to their dogs. Bacteria collect on the tip of the bottle because mills rarely, if ever, clean or replace them. Dogs ingest these bacteria, which causes tooth decay and other health problems. Other puppy mills may provide water to the dogs in buckets and infrequently clean the buckets or change the water. The water becomes slimy and moldy. Eating inferior food contributes to plaque formation and gum disease. By age two, many puppy mill dogs already have rotten teeth and mouth infections.

Many puppy mill breeder dogs also have cracked teeth. Some puppy mill owners "de-bark" their dogs, so that the barking of hundreds of dogs will not disclose their location, by jamming a sharp stick or metal pipe down a dog's throat to rupture their vocal chords. During this incredibly cruel process, some of the dog's teeth may be shattered. Their jaws may be broken, too.

Another reason their teeth get cracked and worn is because these dogs chew on the wire cages that confine them, either in an attempt to escape or to release nervous frustration caused by their continuous confinement. Untreated cracked teeth can also become infected. Quite a few mill dogs' teeth also may be worn down to next to nothing.

Many rescued breeder dogs require teeth extractions and antibiotics to combat these infections. It is not uncommon to meet rescued breeder dogs, such as Buster in chapter five, who have very few or even no teeth at all.

Coat and Skin

Diet and genetics can affect the condition of a dog's coat and skin. Good, quality protein is essential for healthy fur. Without proper nutrition, the coat will not grow as lustrous as it should. Many mill dogs have sparse, dry coats; but after being rescued and fed good, quality food, they can shed these old coats and grow in new ones of more healthy fur. Other mill dogs may never have a nice coat due to genetic in-breeding. Golden Retrievers, for example, would normally have thick undercoats, but I've seen many Goldens rescued from puppy mills who simply don't have this undercoat. I've even seen Poodles and Bichon Frises, breeds with very dense and curly hair, with extremely thin coats.

Infections

Perhaps the harshest reality of puppy mill life is the utter lack of veterinary care. Some puppy mill owners will even perform surgery on their dogs themselves, from tail docking to caesarian sections, without anesthesia and in conditions that are hardly sterile or even safe. Infections almost always result. Of course, since it costs money to treat infections, they are usually left untreated.

In many puppy mills, the dogs' cages are stacked on top of each other. Sadly, I've seen cases where dogs got their limbs caught between the wires on their cages. These dogs may chew on the stuck limb in an attempt to free it, or one of the nearby dogs may use it to chew on, or the mill owner may simply cut it off (often using just a wire cutter). These things really do happen—and more frequently than we want to believe. This is such cruel and terrible suffering.

Mammary Tumors

Because puppy mill females are bred at such a young age (usually at first heat, which is around six months old), are continually bred at every heat, and are never spayed, their propensity for mammary tumors is high. Many times, these tumors are malignant. Dogs stand a good chance of survival if these tumors are identified and treated early. The best way to prevent mammary cancer in dogs is to spay females at an early age (six months is best). However, because puppy mills do not spay their breeding females, rescuers and adopters often spend a great deal of time and money treating the mammary tumors of these unfortunate puppy producers. This is a very common problem.

Parasites

Puppy mill dogs are exposed to just about every kind of parasite imaginable, including worms, fleas, ticks, mites, mange, and even heartworm. Except for mange and heartworm, none of these are fatal, but they still can be very irritating to the dogs' skin and internal systems. Dogs may scratch these itchy bites, and scratching often creates sores and abscesses. Infections are commonplace in puppy mills, and many puppy mill dogs must be treated for parasites after they are rescued.

Ears

In addition to ear mites, most puppy mill dogs have ear infections. Some of these infections are so severe that they leave a black and gooey discharge in the dogs' ears. It smells terrible and the dogs must be in extreme discomfort if not tremendous pain. If the infection becomes severe enough, the dog may lose part or all of their hearing in that ear. But with proper treatment, ear mites and ear infections can be easy to heal.

Eyes

Poor nutrition can also affect a dog's vision. Although not as common as these other health issues, some puppy mill dogs are born blind or lose their eyesight at an early age because they were deprived of essential nutrients, or were nursed by puppy mill mothers who lack these same nutrients. Puppy mill dogs may also have upper respiratory infections that can cause their eyes to weep. The air in many of these mills is so unhealthy from the squalid conditions which also may contribute to their weepy eyes.

Spinning or Pacing

While confined in their puppy mill cages, some dogs become so anxious and distraught that they continually pace or spin around in circles. Their cage may have allowed only just enough space to turn around, and many dogs cannot even stand up in their cages without ducking their heads. Some Lancaster County (PA) puppy mill owners even use rabbit hutches to house their dogs—believe it or not, placing dogs as large as Golden Retrievers and Labrador Retrievers in them. This confinement is too much stress for some dogs to bear. While many dogs simply resign themselves to being imprisoned and withdraw into themselves, others become so nervous and anxious that they must try to work off their anxious and nervous feelings.

Even after they've been rescued and live in more spacious and friendly quarters, some rescued breeder dogs may continue to spin or pace. I've met rescued breeder dogs who were given acres to run free, but continued to pace the exact same length of space to which they were previously confined; if they lived in a cage five feet long, they paced that same five foot space and no more, even though they have complete freedom to run. They simply cannot free themselves of the compulsion to pace caused by their continuous confinement.

Many of these spinners and pacers, like Spin in chapter eight and Buddy in chapter one, recover without intervention. But some may require drug therapy—anti-anxiety medication—to help them overcome this compulsion. Even if this is not quite a physical problem, your rescued mill dog may require veterinary treatment.

Health Issues of Puppy Mill Breeder Dogs

This is the sad and harsh reality for most puppy mill breeder dogs, and animal lovers and consumers must be aware of it. People who adopt a rescued breeder dog need to be fully sympathetic to these challenges. Everyone else who reads this will hopefully think twice before buying that puppy who, no matter how irresistibly adorable, came from a puppy mill.

The following and final chapter describes the health and behavior issues of these puppies produced in puppy mills. Please continue reading.

Puppy Mill Dogs SPEAK!

Chapter Fourteen

HEALTH AND BEHAVIOR ISSUES OF PUPPIES FROM PUPPY MILLS

After learning in the previous chapter about the health and behavior issues of dogs who are the breeding stock in puppy mills, isn't it logical to conclude that the puppies born in these conditions, from these parents, are likely to have health and behavior issues too? After all, puppies depend upon their mothers to provide nutrition while in the womb, and to provide healthy milk and teach them after they are born. If the mother dog is deprived of proper nutrition and natal care, her milk will be deficient and her pups will suffer the consequences. Now that we know that puppy mills are responsible for producing a large majority of puppies in this country, we may already be facing growing numbers of puppies with conditions requiring treatment.

The mother dog's psychological state may impact her pups' behavior as well. It's my observation that more and more dogs are exhibiting behavior issues, ranging from early onset aggression (prior to six months of age) to symptoms of anxiety that manifest in separation anxiety, fears and phobias, and other behavior problems. Anti-anxiety medications previously only used by humans are now regularly prescribed for dogs. This combination of genetic in-breeding, poor nutrition, little positive socialization with people, and being taken away from their mothers too soon (many are taken away at five to six weeks of age), proves toxic to many puppies and most likely contributes to their behavior issues.

Let's take a look at the health issues frequently seen in puppy mill puppies, and then consider these behavior problems.

Health

Due to poor sanitary conditions and lack of veterinary care, puppies produced at mills often carry infectious diseases and parasites. Some diseases are passed along in utero from the mother; others are contracted after the pups are born.

Upper respiratory illnesses such as kennel cough are routinely diagnosed in puppies from puppy mills. Kennel cough is highly contagious, spreads quickly, and is no different from the human cold; if left untreated, kennel cough can lead to deadly pneumonia. Nasal discharge, runny eyes, and general lethargy are telltale signs of these upper respiratory illnesses. People who sell sick puppies often give them antibiotics to cover up these symptoms (of course, the sellers don't give the buyers these medications because they don't want to admit to selling sick puppies), so these health issues only become evident after you've brought your puppy home.

Just about every puppy mill puppy has intestinal parasites passed along from their mothers. Different varieties cause numerous symptoms, ranging from bloody diarrhea to hair loss to anemia and death. People who sell these pups often give their dogs drugs that mask these problems, too.

Some puppy mill puppies suffer from skin diseases such as mange, which can be highly contagious (and much easier for the prospective buyer to notice, because these skin conditions cannot be so easily disguised with medications). Many puppy mill owners will destroy puppies who show signs of mange or other fungal diseases that affect their skin and coat. I was at DVGRR one day when a volunteer brought in a litter of Golden Retrievers: The pups were missing fur on their tails and legs as a result of lying in filth. The puppy mill owner had brought the pups to the vet for treatment (to his credit, because a trip to the vet is rare!). Several pups were responding nicely to the treatment and their fur was growing back, but others required further treatment—and by the time that extra treatment would have taken effect, the pups would no longer be young and cute, and the miller would not get enough money for them. The mill owner was unwilling to spend any more money on these pups, so he ordered the veterinarian to euthanize them. However, the vet refused and ordered the mill owner sign over the pups to him instead. The vet then surrendered the pups to DVGRR who invested the money to properly treat the problem, and then found them great homes!

Another very serious contagious disease is parvovirus. Most pups who contract it die from extreme vomiting, diarrhea, and fever. People who sell these puppies often give them drugs strong enough to mask the symptoms but not enough to cure and save the puppies. It's not unheard of that a pup dies a couple of days after being purchased. Parvovirus is the most common affliction of pet store puppies and the main reason that so many puppies die just a few days after you purchase and bring them home.

Heartworm, carried by mosquitoes, is a fatal disease for canines. Dogs who are bitten by a heartworm-carrying mosquito become infected with worms that lodge in the dog's heart. Left untreated, these worms grow until they impede the blood flow in the heart, and then the dog dies. Prevention—just a monthly pill—is easy. However, many puppy mill owners neglect this preventative in order to save money and make more profit. Symptoms of heartworm include coughing and intolerance to exercise because of the compromised condition of the heart; a dog exhibiting these symptoms can be cured, although treatment can be dangerous if the dog is in poor health.

Finally, quite a few puppy mill puppies have suppressed immune systems, which make them less able to fight off illnesses. Many puppy mills either ship puppies to a distributor who sends them out to the pet stores, or directly to people who sell the puppies (many over the internet). To get puppies to pet stores while they are still at the "cute puppy" stage, they are taken away from their mothers too early, before they are fully weaned, usually at five or six weeks. There are several reasons why the pups' immune systems are weak: By the time the puppies reach their sales points, they will have traveled many, many miles in a large truck loaded with puppies, a journey that often takes a week or two during the time when their immune systems are still developing. The stress of being taken away from the mother and being transported further weakens the puppies. If they were not fully weaned, they also lack the mother's milk necessary for healthy development.

Let's also not overlook the genetic diseases common to dogs from puppy mills: Hip dysplasia, luxating patellae (kneecaps), cataracts, heart murmurs, deafness and epilepsy, to name the most common.

Behavior

I could devote an entire book to the various behavior issues that puppies may manifest as a result of being born and raised improperly in a puppy mill. But that is not the purpose of this book. The intent is to show the realities of puppy mills, and here they are:

Puppies bred in puppy mills are kept in confinement with their mothers, are never let out of their cages, and are not handled regularly enough by humans, at least not enough to give them the positive exposure necessary to trust people (also known as socialization). Puppies' behaviors are shaped a great deal during their first few weeks of life, and their experiences at this time of their lives greatly influence how they react to the world.

Puppies who are not socialized to a variety of people, children, other dogs, sounds, sights or experiences during these critical first sixteen weeks will grow up to fear the very things that he or she was not exposed to. Depending on the dog's personality, some may cower in fear while others might show aggression to the people and things that they were not introduced to as a pup.

Housetraining

Dogs have an in-born instinct not to eliminate in the same area where they sleep and eat. But when confined to puppy mill cages no bigger than their body lengths, they have no choice. Puppies learn from their mothers, and when they see their mothers eliminate right where they live and eat, the puppies will not learn to eliminate elsewhere. When these puppies come into homes, it is not so easy to re-train them to eliminate outside. One of the best ways to house train a dog is to use a crate, but if the pup was already accustomed to eliminating in its crate, then crate training will be of no help. Please follow the techniques described in chapter two.

Anxiety

Anxiety is a genetic condition inherited from one or both parents, but studies have shown that puppies of stressed mothers will be exposed to high levels of the stress hormone cortisol during the pregnancy. According to Dr. Patricia McConnell, "a mother suffering from extreme anxiety puts her offspring at high risk of being anxious and fearful, even as an adult. Apparently, high levels of the stress hormone cortisol produced by the mother result in fewer cortisol receptor cells in the pup (or child or monkey, etc.). This low number of receptor cells means that the pup's brain is unable to perceive and respond to high levels of cortisol in his own body until the system is overloaded with it. Then the brain goes on red alert, sending the emotions into full panic mode, even in situations that would be only mildly stressful for an average individual."[4] I have witnessed this reaction in many, many puppy mill puppies. Some run in fear from the least little thing.

Separation anxiety is a growing issue with America's dogs, one which often requires anti-anxiety medications and behavior rehabilitation. Symptoms of separation anxiety include elimination in the house when the dog's family is absent even though the dog is housetrained, excessive barking, and destructiveness. Many owners are unable to cope with a dog who exhibits these problems: Imagine coming home tired after a hard day's work to find your door scratched and chewed, your carpet soiled, and your neighbors complaining that your dog won't stop barking. Separation anxiety is a common reason why many dogs are surrendered to shelters.

---

[4] McConnell, Patricia B. *The Bark.* "Fear in Dogs—Where does it begin?" Sept/Oct 2009

Aggression

Aggression is a very complicated issue because there are so many different types of and varying causes for aggression. This discussion is not intended to fully explain aggression and how to resolve every problem it can cause, but to alert you to these aggressive behavior problems in puppies from mills.

Veterinary behaviorist Dr. Karen Overall defines aggression as, "within a given context as an appropriate or inappropriate threat or challenge that is ultimately resolved by combat or deference."[5] Threatening gestures include growls, bared teeth and biting attempts. The underlying physical cause of aggression is anxiety, concurrent with the physical production of adrenaline and cortisol in the dog's body. As adrenaline rises in the dog's body, their propensity for aggression increases too.

Food aggression is one of the most common types of aggression you will see in puppy mill puppies. I've worked with eight-week-old pups who will growl and try to bite anyone who comes near their food bowls or bones.

Other types of aggression include possession aggression (sometimes referred to as resource guarding), dog-to-dog aggression, fear aggression and dominance aggression. Of these, fear aggression is also very common in puppy mill pups simply due to genetics, the lack of socialization as pups, or *in utero* conditions, as we discussed above.

Sadly, this is the picture of the new American dog, factory-produced as livestock instead of loving family pets.

[5]Overall, Karen L. (1997). Clinical Behavioral Medicine for Small Animals. St. Louis, Missouri: Mosby, Inc.

Afterword

So, now you know.

After you've been exposed to puppy mill breeder dogs—kept in cages, kept from having their own lives, kept from knowing the joys of companionship and love—it can really make you wonder why people do this to the dogs. It is not a pretty picture, is it? It can really hurt to see.

The thought of adopting one of these rescued breeder dogs may seem hopeless. How could you, or anyone, ever help one of these dogs to become a "normal dog"?

During a support group meeting of puppy mill dog adopters, I was asked to present a timeline for when they could expect their dogs to recover. Everyone who adopts a puppy mill dog wants to know, "How long will it take for them to overcome their fear of strangers?" or "How long will it take to go up and down steps?" I can't give them or anyone any definite answers. It depends. It depends upon how bad the conditions were at the mill. It depends on the personality of your dog. It depends on how much you work with your dog, too.

Adopters have at least one advantage: Dogs are blessedly resilient creatures with a deep, instinctive need to be social. Like some people, they simply love to share love.

Are there characteristics that run through most adopters of breeder dogs? The first is patience. There is no way you'll tolerate the time it takes a rescued breeder dog to work through the issues they need to work through if you don't have patience.

Unconditional love and acceptance of the dog is another. Many dog adopters idealize the image that their adopted dog will walk into their house and be their buddy, walk by their side, lay their head in their laps, be their constant companion. Many people live with rescued breeder dogs that they couldn't touch for weeks or months, which is probably not what they had in mind when they considered adopting a dog. These relationships must be based on unconditional love and acceptance of these dogs just the way they are.

The last thing is a lack of ego. It is so incredibly difficult to not take it personally when you adopt a dog and it does not respond to you. *What did I do? What didn't I do? Why does my dog not like me?* You can easily make this about yourself, but it's not about you. It's about your opportunity: Your amazing opportunity to give another living creature a second chance at life.

But you do not have to adopt a rescued dog in order to help puppy mill breeder dogs. There are other things you can do. Please do not patronize a puppy mill or pet store the next time you buy a dog. This simple act will help decrease the demand for puppy mill dogs.

Most animal rescues and shelters are grateful for donations and volunteers. Many volunteers get to exercise the dogs—this means taking the dogs out to play, which can be a great way to spend a morning, afternoon, or evening.

Afterword

Many states are advancing more humane animal laws, including specific regulatory measures for breeders and puppy mills. If you live in one of these states, let your elected representatives know you want them to support such legislation.

Thousands of dogs live—suffer—right at this moment in situations that seem brutally hopeless. Let's remember that many good and worthwhile things seemed at one point hopeless, too. These courageous dogs and their new families, their successes and setbacks and the thousands more like them, can inspire us to remember that with patience, unconditional love, and lack of ego, nothing is truly hopeless, and anything is possible.

Puppy Mill Dogs SPEAK!

Resources

Agility

—American Kennel Club, www.akc.org/events/agility
—United States Dog Agility Association, www.usdaa.com

Animal Assisted Therapy

—Delta Society, www.deltasociety.org
—Therapy Dogs International, www.tdi-dog.org

Behavior and Training

—*Animals in Translation, Using the Mysteries of Autism to Decode Animal Behavior,* by Dr. Temple Grandin

—Association of Pet Dog Trainers, www.apdt.com

—*Calming Signals, On Talking Terms with Dogs,* by Turid Rugaas

—*Dogs, A Startling New Understanding of Canine Origin, Behavior and Evolution,* by Raymond and Lorna Coppinger

—*How To Speak Dog: Mastering the Art of Dog-Human Communication,* by Stanley Coren

Body Work

—*Canine Massage, A Practical Guide,* by Jean-Pierre Hourdebaigt

—*The Tellington TTouch, A Revolutionary Natural Method to Train and Care for Your Favorite Animal,* by Linda Tellington-Jones

Clicker Training

—Karen Pryor, www.clickertraining.com

Reading with Dogs

—Therapy Animals, Inc., www.therapyanimals.org

Rescue Organizations Featured in This Book

—Brookline Labrador Retriever Rescue:
215-343-6087, www.brooklinelabrescue.org

—Delaware Valley Golden Retriever Rescue:
717-484-4799, www.dvgrr.org

—Main Line Animal Rescue:
610-933-0606, www.mlar.org

Acknowledgements

I don't know how I was led to this career of helping the adopters of puppy mill dogs. I was in the right place at the right time, I suppose, and like a little lost puppy, I faithfully followed where I was being led. Many people and organizations contributed to this journey. Delaware Valley Golden Retriever Rescue was the first organization where I encountered what people called puppy mill dogs, where I became aware that the dogs were from the mills. Certainly, I had previously met mill dogs but other shelters called them "farm dogs" or just "timid dogs." At DVGRR, the staff and adopters and I learned *together* how to best understand and help the mill dogs. Once I started working with these dogs, word seemed to spread that I had the knowledge and understanding to be of assistance.

♥ To the people and their dogs in this book who invited me to tell their stories so that others may learn. They have opened their homes and hearts to these loving and miraculously forgiving yet quirky canines. Ann Metcalf was one of the first of these adopters. Through Penny, her Golden Retriever breeder dog, Ann and I began a project to document the rehabilitation of puppy mill dogs in film. Ann's film *Uncaged, Second Chances for Puppy Mills Breeder Dogs* first aired on television in March, 2008 and continues to be aired. We hope through this project that we enlightened many people to the plight of our dog friends. I thank Ann for inviting me to work with her.

♥ To the people who tirelessly dedicate themselves to freeing the dogs from the mills—DVGRR, Main Line Animal Rescue, Brookline Labrador Retriever Rescue and many, many others. I hope that you are eventually put out of business!

♥ To Chris Slawecki, not just for his superior editorial and writing skills but for the moral support he gave me when I became discouraged. It was no accident that we were brought together. To Jodi Mossie who gave her time and talents to design the beautiful and inspiring graphics for this book. To Donna Baker who used her brilliant editorial skills to lend "another set of eyes" and for her moral support. To Deb Bock for her perfection with the final phase of layout and design.

♥ To my family and friends who doubted my sanity when I quit my 25-year career in telecommunications to work with animals. Thank you for not giving up on me!

♥ Lastly, to my own dogs, living and long gone: Reve, Caper, Gizzy, Donner and Archie. I wish that everyone has the blessing of knowing this kind of love, and I trust there are many more in my future.

—*Chris Shaughness*

Acknowledgements

♥ ♥ ♥ ♥ ♥ ♥ ♥

♥ First thanks to Chris Shaughness, who had no good reason for accepting my contribution to this book other than the fact that I asked her to. The trust you've shown in me and the miles that we've walked together have been an honor.

♥ Second thanks to someone I have never met and do not even know. In July 2007, someone delivered a breeder dog rescued from a puppy mill to Delaware Valley Golden Retriever Rescue, who helped Buster find his way home to us. Whoever you are: Your act of simple humane kindness changed more than that dog's life; you profoundly changed my life and helped me to see things in the world and in myself that I had never seen before. Thank you so much.

♥ Many thanks to the staff and volunteers at Brookline Rescue, Delaware Valley Golden Retriever Rescue, and Main Line Animal Rescue, and to the thousands of people all around the world just like them, all of whom earn their wings every single day.

♥ Many, many thanks to my family and friends at home and at church and at work. Not one of you has run away when I've gotten "that look" when talking about these dogs or this book. Thank you for listening and for caring.

♥ Ultimate thanks to a wise God who knew that we would need a warm, living reflection of His loyalty, forgiveness, and compassion here on earth, held a mirror up to His own face, and taught us how to spell His name backwards.

—*Chris Slawecki*

Made in the USA
Monee, IL
14 November 2020